The Psychosocial Reality of Digital Travel

"A common approach today in book-length human-oriented treatments of new digital technologies is to jump right in and start discussing issues as if there were no previous theoretical works worthy of systematic consideration. Tjostheim and Waterworth try another tack in *The Psychosocial Reality of Digital Travel*. Their text contains a careful selection of theoretical perspectives for the key issues they discuss. What a difference that makes! Their combination of theoretical insights with user studies and critical analysis makes for an excellent read. Reading this book can help further one's own thinking with regards to the emerging new area of digital travel, as well as to virtual reality and presence research, place theory, the philosophy of perception and a host of other related topics, in a way that can only happen when elements of theory, empirical work, and analysis support each other meaningfully."
—Anders Hedman, *Associate Professor, KTH Royal Institute of Technology, Sweden*

"Can virtual travels become as attractive as real ones? In this insightful book, Tjostheim and Waterworth suggest that although a digital journey differs from a 'physical' one in many respects, it can be a rich and satisfying experience, provided that it enables the traveller to achieve a high sense of 'presence' – the feeling of 'being there.' However, as the authors convincingly show, creating presence is not just a technological challenge: imagination, expectations, and the story or narrative through which the traveller makes sense of the journey also play a key role."
—Andrea Gaggioli, *Professor, Director of the ExperienceLab, Università Cattolica del Sacro Cuore, Italy*

"This book offers an original and informative interpretation of travel in the electronically permeated world in which we now live. I was particularly intrigued by the authors' development of the idea of behavioural outsideness as an aspect of digital experiences of place. Virtual travel may not be a substitute for visiting somewhere, but this book shows that the increasingly realistic 3D rendering of places in digital games and other tele-technologies does provide a powerful affirmation of actual travel experiences."
—Edward Relph, *Emeritus Professor, Department of Geography and Planning, University of Toronto, Canada*

Ingvar Tjostheim · John A. Waterworth

The Psychosocial Reality of Digital Travel

Being in Virtual Places

Ingvar Tjostheim
Norwegian Computing Center
Oslo, Norway

John A. Waterworth
Department of Informatics
Umeå University
Umeå, Sweden

ISBN 978-3-030-91271-0   ISBN 978-3-030-91272-7 (eBook)
https://doi.org/10.1007/978-3-030-91272-7

© The Editor(s) (if applicable) and The Author(s) 2022. This book is an open access publication.

Open Access This book is licensed under the terms of the Creative Commons Attribution 4.0 International License (http://creativecommons.org/licenses/by/4.0/), which permits use, sharing, adaptation, distribution and reproduction in any medium or format, as long as you give appropriate credit to the original author(s) and the source, provide a link to the Creative Commons license and indicate if changes were made.

The images or other third party material in this book are included in the book's Creative Commons license, unless indicated otherwise in a credit line to the material. If material is not included in the book's Creative Commons license and your intended use is not permitted by statutory regulation or exceeds the permitted use, you will need to obtain permission directly from the copyright holder.

The use of general descriptive names, registered names, trademarks, service marks, etc. in this publication does not imply, even in the absence of a specific statement, that such names are exempt from the relevant protective laws and regulations and therefore free for general use.

The publisher, the authors and the editors are safe to assume that the advice and information in this book are believed to be true and accurate at the date of publication. Neither the publisher nor the authors or the editors give a warranty, expressed or implied, with respect to the material contained herein or for any errors or omissions that may have been made. The publisher remains neutral with regard to jurisdictional claims in published maps and institutional affiliations.

Cover illustration: © Harvey Loake

This Palgrave Macmillan imprint is published by the registered company Springer Nature Switzerland AG
The registered company address is: Gewerbestrasse 11, 6330 Cham, Switzerland

Contents

1	**Introduction**	1
	Why Digital Travel?	2
	The Mind of the Digital Traveller	4
	A Roadmap for the Book	8
	References	10
2	**Being Somewhere**	13
	Introduction	14
	The Nature of Experiences, and of Experiences of Other Places	15
	The Philosophy of Perceptual Experience	16
	Four Philosophical Views on the Nature of Perceptual Experiences	17
	The Representational View	18
	Relationism	21
	Enactivism	22
	The Sense-data View	24
	Summary of the Four Theories	26
	Dual Process Theories and Intuitive Judgment	29
	The Spinozan Model of Rapid Acceptance Response	29
	Everyday Activities in the World: Transparency and Embodiment	31
	Heidegger and Modes of Engaging with the World	32
	Transparency	34

	Embodiment	35
	Presence and the Direct Perception Approach	38
	Summary and Conclusions	40
	References	41
3	**Feeling Present in Virtual Environments**	51
	Introduction	52
	Conceptualisations of Telepresence: Being Present at a Distance	55
	The Illusion *of non-Mediation*	55
	Pretending the Digital Is Physical	56
	Experiencing a Convincing Simulated Semblance (of Physical Reality)	57
	Telepresence and Perceptual Illusions	58
	Perception, Imagination and Attention	61
	Presence as the Feeling of Attending to a Surrounding External World	62
	Social Interaction and Affordances for Presence	63
	Interacting with Other People	63
	Activities in Place: The Role of Affordances	64
	Implications For Digital Travel	67
	References	68
4	**Visiting Places**	73
	Introduction	73
	Sense of Place	75
	Spaces and Places	75
	Human Geography and Edwards Relph's Place Theory	75
	Marketing and Hedonic Consumption	78
	Intention to Visit a Place and Word of Mouth	80
	Experiencing Sense of Place in a Virtual Environment	80
	Insights from Non-digital Travel and Tourism	82
	Conclusions	83
	References	85
5	**The Reality of Digital Travel**	93
	Introduction	93
	Digital Travel and Sense of Place	96
	The Use of Video Games and Photo-Realism	97
	Creating a Sightseeing Experience in a Video Game	99

	A Virtual Visit to Los Angeles	100
	The Sightseers' Experience of Telepresence and Sense of Place	101
	Results—Virtual Sightseers Had the Feeling of Being There in the City	103
	Digital Travel Applications—A Survey on Behaviours and Attitudes	106
	Conclusions	123
	References	123
6	**When the Virtual Becomes Real?**	129
	Introduction	129
	Recent Innovations in Digital Travel	131
	Social Telepresence Robots and Drones	132
	Immersive VR Approaches and the Use of Holograms	133
	Rethinking Digital Travel	135
	Metaphors and the Blending of Physical-Digital Realities	135
	Reflecting on Our Journey so Far, and Our Plans	139
	References	144

Index   149

List of Figures

Fig. 2.1	The disposition to accept propositions—The Spinozan model	30
Fig. 2.2	Heidegger and modes of engaging in the world	33
Fig. 2.3	Dasein and levels of abstraction	34
Fig. 3.1	A section of Castellum umbrarum (Giovanni Fontana, 1420, Bayerische Staatsbibliothek)	54
Fig. 3.2	The Müller-Lyer illusion and the Necker cube	59
Fig. 5.1	How the participants experienced Los Angeles measured with three alternative measurements	103
Fig. 5.2	Los Angeles—the feeling of being there	104
Fig. 5.3	Los Angeles—perceptual realism and affordances	105
Fig. 5.4	The effect of the digital experience on the need for travel planning	106
Fig. 5.5	The participants—age and gender	107
Fig. 5.6	The participants—age and education	108
Fig. 5.7	Experience with digital meetings	108
Fig. 5.8	Frequency of holiday travel per year	109
Fig. 5.9	Travel planning 2021	110
Fig. 5.10	Holiday destinations	110
Fig. 5.11	The vaccination and age-groups	111
Fig. 5.12	Private vaccination and travel	112
Fig. 5.13	Sources of geographical information and information that can create a sense of place	112
Fig. 5.14	The use travel apps or virtual presentations	113
Fig. 5.15	Digital presentations of museums or other attractions	114

Fig. 5.16	Museums and other attractions—the digital experience in comparison to the in situ experience	115
Fig. 5.17	Digital presentations of a hotel	116
Fig. 5.18	Digital presentations of activities	116
Fig. 5.19	Activities—the digital experience in comparison to the in situ experience	117
Fig. 5.20	Digital presentations of guided tours	118
Fig. 5.21	Guided tours—the digital experience in comparison to the in situ experience	118
Fig. 5.22	Digital travel applications for sharing and re-experience the vacation	119
Fig. 5.23	Digital travel applications in the future—expectations	119
Fig. 5.24	Willingness to pay for digital travel pro	120
Fig. 5.25	Willingness to pay for digital travel products – a comparison to ticket prices of a service at the travel destination	121
Fig. 5.26	Arguments for digital travel	121
Fig. 5.27	Digital travel—a substitute for the in situ experience	122
Fig. 5.28	The digital travel experience—similar to the in situ experience?	122
Fig. 6.1	Designing with blends	137

List of Tables

Table 2.1	Representationalism, relationism, enactivism and the sense datum theory	27
Table 2.2	Characteristics of System 1 and System 2 thinking	31
Table 4.1	Relph's seven types of place experience	77
Table 4.2	Framework for evaluating the extent to which a digital travel experience can be seen as an actual travel experience (bold indicates the most relevant)	84
Table 4.3	Relph's types of sense of place with two new types of outsideness	85
Table 6.1	Blending applied to the metaphor "To use my device is to be a traveller"	138

CHAPTER 1

Introduction

Abstract When physical travel to a specific place is prohibited or otherwise difficult or impossible, digital travel provides a promising alternative. The technology to do this is now widely available and many people have the possibility to meet with others digitally, and thus alleviate the social effects of physical isolation. Digital travel can also be source of pleasure and entertainment, and many people spend time exploring and interacting in digital places, realistically rendering in 3D games. But despite the recent upsurge in virtual social interaction, it does not meet many of the psychosocial aspects of the travel experience. In this book, we take a fresh look at the nature of the telepresence experience in digital environments. We also address a number of relevant questions, such as whether these experiences can seem real to the digital traveller and, if so, under what conditions and on what grounds.

Keywords Travel · Tourism · Videoconferencing · Covid-19 · Virtuality · Cyberspace

© The Author(s) 2022
I. Tjostheim and J. A. Waterworth, *The Psychosocial Reality of Digital Travel*,
https://doi.org/10.1007/978-3-030-91272-7_1

Why Digital Travel?

The history of travel goes hand in hand with the history of humanity. Travel and tourism are many-faceted, and can be studied using methods from many research traditions. Very few researchers, or people in general, use the terms digital travel or virtual travel, even though conditions in our societies differ significantly from the recent past. Understanding what these terms mean needs to draw on a range of contexts and research traditions, which is what we have attempted to do in this book. In tourism research, for example, the focus is often on the experience, what travellers do and where they go (the destinations of travel). Telepresence research, a relatively new research area, often concerns how to understand why we have a feeling of being there, in a virtual place, and how to measure this experience, but this has not often been framed as *digital travel*.

People increasingly travel, visit and meet other people digitally in computer-mediated environments. The covid-19 pandemic, and the restrictions on physical meetings and travel that have come with it, has resulted in an enormous change in behaviour and attitudes towards the practicality and acceptability of replacing physical encounters with virtual ones. Prior to this, videoconferencing and other technologies were already used in business and as a way for families and friends to keep in touch over distances. Recent developments have led to many other kinds of meetings and events taking place without physical travel; for example, concerts, school and college classes, sports events, academic and other conferences, training and personal development courses and medical consultations.

Many computer games use realistically presented (distant) places as the venue for action. These may be fictional, but are often digital versions of actual physical places, such as museums, famous localities, sports stadiums, motor racetracks, cities and so on. In these and other virtual environments, the visitor may explore and sightsee in ways that are somewhat analogous to being a tourist in a physical location. But there are significant differences between being a virtual tourist and physically travelling for pleasure to places people live and work, as a tourist traditionally does.

To travel to a particular place at a particular time has always been important for people. When physical travel to a specific place is prohibited or otherwise difficult or impossible, virtual travel provides a promising alternative. If we cannot go to an event and meet our friends, colleagues or new acquaintances there, we can still meet via a teleconference system, in a virtual room. The technology to do this is now widely available and many people have the possibility to meet with others in virtuality, and so overcome—or at least alleviate—the social effects of physical isolation, which is known to be detrimental to both physical and mental wellbeing. But despite the recent upsurge in virtual social interaction, many people feel that they are missing something important—the travel experience, visiting places and meeting people face to face. And there is evidence that such virtual interactions can be stressful and more tiring than their physical counterparts.

The experience of physical place is also undergoing profound changes, through the widespread adoption of mobile technology and, in particular, the almost universal use of mobile phones. The way mobile phones are used has been compared to a snail carrying its home on its back. Being able to attend to the phone, and via the phone to distant people and places, can provide a "home" into which we can retreat or return. Wherever we are, however socially dull or difficult that place may be, we can always take out our phone and "escape". A recent study (Miller et al., 2021) found that users across many age groups feel about their phones in analogous ways to how they about their homes. In an interview with the Guardian newspaper (*Guardian*, May 13, 2021) one of the authors, Daniel Miller commented that *"The smartphone is no longer just a device that we use, it's become the place where we live. The flip side of that for human relationships is that at any point, whether over a meal, a meeting or other shared activity, a person we're with can just disappear, having 'gone home' to their smartphone"*. The possibility to mentally leave one's current social situation is referred to in the study as the "death of proximity" in face-to-face interactions. These developments can be seen as making the difference between physical and digital travel less striking.

Meetings between people increasingly take place in virtual spaces, via teleconferencing systems such as Zoom, Teams and Skype. But these meetings do not always satisfy the needs of the attendees, and may lead to fatigue, to some extent by violating social interaction norms. For example, in a typical working configuration at home, with a personal computer with embedded camera, the people with which we meet may appear too close for comfort, and we are also not used to seeing ourselves during meetings in a way that may make us overly self-conscious (Bailenson, 2021).

Meyrowitz (1986) made the case that modern communication media lack the sense of place that frames the social behaviours of the people interacting within and through them. In these environments, people have what seem to be face-to-face encounters, and yet they are not, since the participants are in different physical places and do not share the real experience of being in the same place. Meyrowitz' vision was prescient, and speaks directly to our intensely and increasingly media-networked relationships. We have "friends" on Facebook, for example, with people we have never physically met, never shared the experience of an actual place with. We meet them, but our meetings lack something vital to human encounters—a real sense of *travel* to actual *places*. Relph (2021) talks about widespread "digital disorientation" produced by the characteristics of participatory and globally networked communication media. As he comments: "The arduous and abrasive situations, discordance, speeding up, and phantasmagoric mixing of cultural memories that are symptoms of digital disorientation flourish in this quintessentially placeless environment". (Relph, 2021, p. 574). And this disorientation is not limited to digital interactions. Relph (2021) goes on to suggest that "because participants in the web are also inhabitants of the material world, these disruptions can come back to invade experiences of actual places". Physical places are altered by digital encounters in cyberspace, a point to which we return in later chapters.

The Mind of the Digital Traveller

In his book on travel, The Mind of the Traveler (Leed, 1991) Eric Leed identifies and provides historical, sociological and psychological insights about the different elements that together combine to form a *journey*, carried out by a *traveller*. A journey consists of departure, passage and arrival; each has its own characteristics and significance. *Departure* is not only about leaving a place, no longer being there, but also involves a change in the psyche, in the self. The traveller not only leaves a place, he leaves a part of his identity by adopting another. For a few, the *passage* from one place to another is an end in itself—the reason for travelling is not to arrive somewhere, but to be in transit. But for most travellers, the passage marks a process of transition, personal as well as physical, from one place to another. It may be slow or fast, comfortable or arduous, safe or hazardous, but it is always a process, a change marked by its own character and imprinted on the traveller. In an *arrival*, the traveller is either a stranger, or is coming home from a strange, a different, place. Arriving is often risky: how does this place work? Will I be accepted? Have things changed since last I was here? How should I behave?

Tourism scholars have extensively discussed the question of why people travel and the tourist experience. Many scholars and authors have contributed to our understanding of travel, holidays and leisure activities and to see tourism as "a temporary reversal of everyday activities", as expressed by Cohen (1979), who identified several different modes of tourism experience (to which we return later in Chapter 4). Tourism can be characterised as a "home-away-back-home" journey. The nature of tourism is that it involves both a going out, from home, and a return to home. Nowadays, tourism is a huge industry, with broad economic impact on countries around the world. But, more importantly, it has become a part of the personal life of most people. A tourist has a desire to visit places and to visually appreciate sights. The essence of tourism is visual consumption, "the tourist gaze" (Urry, 1990, 1992a, 1992b). It is often mediated through a camera; still photographic images or videos. The tourist then views the world at a distance and, at its extreme, travel is a strategy for the accumulation of photographs (Urry, 1990: 139) to be viewed and shared, or just filed away. The notion of the tourist gaze emphasises a person's mental distance from a remote place. "*The post-tourist knows that they are a tourist and that tourism is a game, or rather a whole series of games with multiple texts and no single, authentic tourist experience*" (Urry, 1990: 100; cf. Turner et al., 2005). Urry emphasises the visual; tourists visit "*sights*" and enjoy seeing places.

Virtual tourism and VR for tourism can be traced back to the early 1990s (Bauer and Jacobsen, 1995; Benjamin & Cooper, 1995; Cheong, 1995; Dewailly, 1999; Williams & Hobson, 1995). In the 1990s, research on virtual tourism was primarily conducted by IT-researchers and it was anticipated that virtual tourism would become a mainstream knowledge domain for adoption by the tourism industry. We are not there yet. Some also investigated the relationship between virtual tourism and actual travelling, seeing the former as a potential marketing tool.

Fencott (1999) and Fencott et al. (2003) argued that the longer visitors linger overall in a virtual tourism environment, the more likely they are to find the virtual experience memorable and perhaps retain the desire to actually visit the place the VE is modelling. Williams (2006) discusses how technology can produce virtual visits, and some implications for tourism of a virtual visit. Losh (2006) describes how the serious game *Virtual Iraq* can be used to trigger memories and stimulate coping mechanisms in combat veterans suffering from Post-Traumatic Stress Disorder, an example of a wide range of similar work capitalising on the psychotherapeutic potential of VR. This potential is presumably based on similarities between experiencing the VR and experiencing the actual situation in physical reality. Widyarto and Latiff (2007) emphasise that a virtual application works well in a travel context as a tool for getting to know the place and navigation purposes, but they also argued that it cannot replace the real-world experience.

It might be that a tourist does not accept a virtual substitute, but exposure to the virtual place may nevertheless increase their desire to visit the actual place (Dewailly, 1999). According to Beck et al. (2019) there are studies that suggest that VR, regardless of whether it is non-, semi- or fully immersive, is capable of positively influencing an individual's motivation to actually visit a place. According to Plunkett (2011) a virtual experience can create an attachment to a place, and this may not be to the place as displayed on the screen, but to the physical place it represents. Tourism is, for good reasons, of interest to telepresence research because the tourist experience is a multisensory experience (Rickly-Boyd, 2009) and because the "there" in *being there* (a characterisation of telepresence) can be a tourist destination.

The "there" in the *being there* of telepresence and the "there" of actually visiting and experiencing a place in travel and tourism is a red thread running through the structure of this book. Each chapter addresses both perspectives; physical being and virtual being. In telepresence the "being there" is in most cases relatively short or "in the moment", while physical travel and tourist experiences are longer and do not evaporate when we have breaks in presence—a sudden glitch, power outage or simply turning off the device we are using.

In situ, for instance, as a tourist at holiday destination, we do not think about whether where we are is real or not. But when we play a digital game, this factor has an effect. Schwartz (2006) argues that realism and attention to detail allow gamers to experience game spaces as real. As an example, he quotes a player of the video game *Grand Theft Auto*: "*You feel as if you're in a real town/city with other people*" (p. 315). From observations such as this, it can be inferred that some gamers visit and explore a game space in a manner similar to tourists exploring a physical space. Schwartz concludes that video game environments afford the blending of fantasy and realistic aspects into a believable, attractive place for players to visit.

In his review article on virtual tourism, Guttentag (2010) discusses many aspects of relevance for the tourism industry. He observes that virtual tours are often panoramic photographs that do not permit any free navigation, meaning that they are not what he describes as genuine

VR—explorable 3D spaces (Guttentag, 2010). Surprisingly, there seems to be very little overlap between the telepresence literature and the virtual tourism literature (Yung & Khoo-Lattimore, 2019). Guttentag (2010) cites only three papers from the two leading journals on telepresence; two papers from *Presence: Teleoperators and Virtual Environments* and one paper from *Cyberpsychology, Behaviour and Social Networking*. This indicates that very few tourism researchers have built on telepresence research. There is one noticeable exception; the authors of the publications from the Benogo project explicitly link tourism and telepresence (Turner et al., 2013), and human geography to experiences in VEs (O'Neill, 2005; Benyon et al., 2006; Turner & Turner, 2006; Turner et al., 2005). This is in line with the mission of the project; Benogo stands for "Be there without going there". Clearly, virtual tourism is related to telepresence since both concern the feeling of *being there*.

The telepresence researcher Mel Slater does not discuss tourism per se, but emphasises the idea of *place* in *being there*. He writes: *"this 'experiencing-as-a-place' is very much what I have tried to convey as a meaning of presence in VEs: people are 'there', they respond to what is 'there', and they remember it as a 'place'"* (Slater, 1999: 562). In a more recent paper, Slater and Sanchez-Vives (2016) discuss virtual travel with reference to Cheong's (1995) visions for virtual tourism in the mid-1990s. They conclude the section by writing (p. 27); *"Perhaps, VR is not meant to be a substitute for real travel but just another form of travel, no less valid in its own terms than all that physically boarding the real aeroplane entails"*.

A study by Lombard and Weinstein (2012) has a quote from a person who filled in the *Telepresence Experience Survey*, a survey instrument designed to let the participants use their own words to describe different types of (tele)presence experience. One of the participants wrote *"I completely felt that I was a part of the world and the characters and settings were all real and places I have been", (p. 6)*. The quote indicates that the person had a strong virtual tourism experience.

In tourism research some refer to the telepresence concept, but there remains a dearth of empirical work, including using ways of measuring telepresence. Gretzel (2011: 758) observes that while science and technology studies have permeated other fields, it is absent from mainstream tourism literature. One of the aims in the book is to correct this lack in the literature.

In what follows, we take a fresh look at the nature of the telepresence experience in digital environments, at a time when more and more people are engaged in meetings and other interactive experiences within virtual environments (VEs) of one kind or another. We also address a number of relevant questions, such as whether these experiences can seem real to the virtual traveller and, if so, under what conditions and on what grounds? And more generally to what extent can technology be designed to make up for the needs that physical travel fills, in light of findings on physical and social presence in virtual environments?

Can a "home-away-back-home" metaphor derived from tourism be usefully applied to virtual travel, for example? Can virtual spaces become true social places that satisfy the requirements for host–guest interactions, and become fulfilling destinations for travel? We know that interactive technology can be used to create a convincing fantasy world, and also to replicate a place that actually exists. If a VR environment replicates a place that a person can visit, what experience is created and how can we understand it? This is an underlying theme in the book and is directly related to our choice for discussion of theories and findings from a range of fields, including philosophy, psychology and social science, telepresence research, human geography and tourism studies.

A Roadmap for the Book

Having outlined and briefly discussed relevant concepts related to virtual spaces and digital travel in this chapter, we move on to consider in more detail the feeling of "being there" for the quality and success of virtual social interactions and travels to distant (or fictional) places. We start in Chapter 2 by examining what is known about the sense of being *somewhere*, using arguments based on relevant theories of embodiment, perception, action and social behaviour. We think this largely philosophical overview is helpful in understanding the material to be covered later, especially with regard to presence, perceptual illusions and being in places. Readers not wishing to go so deeply into these aspects may prefer to take a shortcut to Chapter 3 and beyond.

In Chapter 3, we compare and contrast different current theoretical accounts of telepresence, in the light of their plausibility and implications for understanding in what ways people can experience a sense of being in other places, with other people, using digital technology; how, through digital technology, we can have a sense of being *somewhere else*.

Next, in Chapter 4, we examine different notions of place, as outlined in work in tourism studies and other applied social fields; how and when different experiences of place arise for the traveller, and the distinction between spaces and places and their respective characteristics and roles in social interactions. We also look closely at a neglected topic in the literature: How do telepresence and the sense of place relate to each other?

Chapter 5 summarises and interprets findings from two sets of recent empirical studies of the authors on digital travel. The first was on factors affecting the sense of place experience, and telepresence, using video games to create a sightseeing environment for participants. The second was a survey of a broad sample of citizens on their attitudes to vacation planning and digital travel applications used before, during and after visiting a tourist destination. We found that some respondents expect to have digital travel experiences in the future, experiences that we can describe as digital visits to a place without travelling physically.

Chapter 6 addresses the question of how we can design for virtual travel and meetings, so that the experience is more satisfying, and real, for participants. We selectively present current interactive design trends and possibilities for a future in which more and more travel is virtual rather than physical, in the light of the arguments and findings presented earlier in the book. For example: Is it possible to maintain key role-related aspects of behaviour in appropriately designed virtual, or mixed reality spaces? What would this entail? Can the physical and the virtual be blended to support embodied interaction in integrated places that span distant boundaries? If such places can become real for the participants, not only in the moment, but as lasting, memorable experiences of being there, real virtual travel could then replace the currently disjointed social interactions through the Internet that have become so familiar.

We complete our journey through this book by concluding our argument that the feeling one is actually in a place—the feeling of "being there"—is vital to the quality and success of virtual social interactions and travels to distant (or fictional) places. This is especially relevant at times when travel is restricted or prohibited, since a lack of travel can mean few social opportunities, leading to a sense of isolation and sometimes depression. Currently, however, virtual travel is unlike physical travel in many significant respects, and does not adequately satisfy the sociopsychological needs of people meeting, of tourists and their hosts, or of other kinds of travellers. We draw together our conclusions and present speculations about the not-too-distant future, when digital travel may become truly real.

References

Bailenson, J. N. (2021). Nonverbal overload: A theoretical argument for the causes of Zoom fatigue. *Technology, Mind, and Behavior, 2*(1). https://doi.org/10.1037/tmb0000030

Bauer, C., & Jacobson, R. (1995). Virtual travel: Promoting tourism to unfamiliar sites through pre-trip experience. In *Information and communication technologies in tourism (ENTER '95)* (pp. 17–21). Springer-Verlag.

Beck, J., Rainoldi, M., & Egger, R. (2019). Virtual reality in tourism: A state-of-the-art review. *Tourism Review, 74*(3), 586–612. https://doi.org/10.1108/TR-03-2017-0049

Benjamin, I., & Cooper, M. (1995). Virtual tourism—A realistic assessment of virtual reality for the tourist industry. In *Information and communication technologies in tourism (ENTER' 95)* (pp. 135–143). Springer-Verlag.

Benyon, D., Smyth, M., O'Neill, S., McCall, R., & Carroll, F. (2006). The place probe: Exploring a sense of place in real and virtual environments. *Presence: Teleoperators and Virtual Environments, 15*(6), 668–687. https://doi.org/10.1162/pres.15.6.668

Cheong, R. (1995). The virtual threat to travel and tourism. *Tourism Management, 16*(6), 417–422. https://doi.org/10.1016/0261-5177(95)00049-T

Cohen, E. (1979). Rethinking the sociology of tourism. *Annals of Tourism Research, 6*(1), 18–35. https://doi.org/10.1016/0160-7383(79)90092-6

Dewailly, J. (1999). Sustainable tourist space: From reality to virtual reality? *Tourism Geographies, 1*(1), 41–55. https://doi.org/10.1080/14616689908721293

Fencott, C., van Schaik, P., Ling, J., & Shafiullah, M. (2003). The effects of movement of attractors and pictorial content of rewards on users' behaviour in virtual environments: An empirical study in the framework of perceptual opportunities. *Interacting with Computers, 15*(1), 121–140. https://doi.org/10.1016/S0953-5438(02)00030-9

Fencott, C. (1999). Content and creativity in virtual environments design. In *Proceedings, proceedings of virtual systems and multimedia* (pp. 308–317). University of Abertay Dundee.

Gretzel, U. (2011). Intelligent systems in tourism. *Annals of Tourism Research, 38*(3), 757–779. https://doi.org/10.1016/j.annals.2011.04.014

Guttentag, D. A. (2010). Virtual reality: Applications and implications for tourism. *Tourism Management, 31*(5), 637–651. https://doi.org/10.1016/j.tourman.2009.07.003

Leed, E. J. (1991). *The mind of the traveler: From Gilgamesh to global tourism*. Basic books.
Lombard, M., & Weinstein, L. (2012). What are telepresence experiences like in the real world? A qualitative survey. In *Proceedings, the 14th International Society for Presence Research (ISPR)*.
Losh, E. (2006). The palace of memory: Virtual tourism and tours of duty in tactical Iraqi and virtual Iraq. In *Proceedings of the 2006 international conference on game research and development* (pp. 77–86). Murdoch University.
Meyrowitz, J. (1986). *No sense of place: The impact of electronic media on social behavior* (1. issued as an Oxford University Press paperback). Oxford University Press.
Miller, D. (2021). *The global smartphone: Beyond a youth technology*. UCL Press. https://doi.org/10.14324/111.9781787359611
O'Neill, S. (2005). Presence. *Place and the Virtual Spectacle. Psychnology, 3*(2), 149–161.
Plunkett, D. (2011). On place attachments in virtual worlds. *World Leisure Journal, 53*(3), 168–178. https://doi.org/10.1080/04419057.2011.606825
Relph, E. (2021). Digital disorientation and place. *Memory Studies, 14*(3), 572–577. https://doi.org/10.1177/17506980211010694
Rickly-Boyd, J. M. (2009). The tourist narrative. *Tourist Studies, 9*(3), 259–280. https://doi.org/10.1177/1468797610382701
Schwartz, L. (2006). Fantasy, realism, and the other in recent video games. *Space and Culture, 9*(3), 313–325. https://doi.org/10.1177/1206331206289019
Slater, M. (1999). Measuring presence: A response to the Witmer and Singer presence questionnaire. *Presence: Teleoperators and Virtual Environments, 8*(5), 560–565. https://doi.org/10.1162/105474699566477
Slater, M., & Sanchez-Vives, M. V. (2016). Enhancing our lives with immersive virtual reality. *Frontiers in Robotics and A, 1*, 3. https://doi.org/10.3389/frobt.2016.00074
Smartphone is now 'the place where we live'. (2021, May 10). https://www.theguardian.com/technology/2021/may/10/smartphone-is-now-the-place-where-we-live-anthropologists-say
Turner, P., & Turner, S. (2006). Place, sense of place, and presence. *Presence: Teleoperators and Virtual Environments, 15*(2), 204–217. https://doi.org/10.1162/pres.2006.15.2.204
Turner, P., Turner, S., & Burrows, L. (2013). Creating a sense of place with a deliberately constrained virtual environment. *International Journal of Cognitive Performance Support, 1*(1), 54. https://doi.org/10.1504/IJCPS.2013.053554
Turner, P., Turner, S., & Carroll, F. (2005). The tourist gaze: Towards contextualised virtual environments. In P. Turner & E. Davenport (Eds.), *Spaces,*

spatiality and technology (Vol. 5, pp. 281–297). Springer-Verlag. https://doi.org/10.1007/1-4020-3273-0_19

Urry, J. (1990). The 'consumption' of tourism. *Sociology, 24*(1), 23–35. https://doi.org/10.1177/0038038590024001004

Urry, J. (1992). The tourist gaze and the 'environment'. *Theory, Culture & Society, 9*(3), 1–26. https://doi.org/10.1177/026327692009003001

Urry, J. (1992). The tourist gaze "revisited." *American Behavioral Scientist, 36*(2), 172–186. https://doi.org/10.1177/0002764292036002005

Widyarto, S., Abd, S., & Latiff, M. (2007). The use of virtual tours for cognitive preparation of visitors: A case study for VHE. *Facilities, 25*(7/8), 271–285. https://doi.org/10.1108/02632770710753316

Williams, A. (2006). Tourism and hospitality marketing: Fantasy, feeling and fun. *International Journal of Contemporary Hospitality Management, 18*(6), 482–495. https://doi.org/10.1108/09596110610681520

Williams, P., & Hobson, J. P. (1995). Virtual reality and tourism: Fact or fantasy? *Tourism Management, 16*(6), 423–427. https://doi.org/10.1016/0261-5177(95)00050-X

Yung, R., & Khoo-Lattimore, C. (2019). New realities: A systematic literature review on virtual reality and augmented reality in tourism research. *Current Issues in Tourism, 22*(17), 2056–2081. https://doi.org/10.1080/13683500.2017.1417359

Open Access This chapter is licensed under the terms of the Creative Commons Attribution 4.0 International License (http://creativecommons.org/licenses/by/4.0/), which permits use, sharing, adaptation, distribution and reproduction in any medium or format, as long as you give appropriate credit to the original author(s) and the source, provide a link to the Creative Commons license and indicate if changes were made.

The images or other third party material in this chapter are included in the chapter's Creative Commons license, unless indicated otherwise in a credit line to the material. If material is not included in the chapter's Creative Commons license and your intended use is not permitted by statutory regulation or exceeds the permitted use, you will need to obtain permission directly from the copyright holder.

CHAPTER 2

Being Somewhere

Abstract To understand the experience of being present somewhere else, via a digital environment, we start by considering how we can experience being anywhere. We present several different philosophical and psychological perspectives on this, stressing the importance of perception. Each has something to offer and add to our understanding of digital travel. We compare four philosophical views: representationalism, relationism, enactivism and the sense-data view. Each has its strengths and weaknesses, but relationism is best placed to accommodate perceptual illusions, which is a prevalent view of the psychological nature of telepresence experiences. As suggested by enactivism and the direct perception approach, the possibilities for action in the world are important to the nature of our experience of places. This, in turn, is influenced by the characteristics of the world in which we act, through affordances.

Keywords Being-in-the-world · Perception · Enactivism · Telepresence · Transparency

Introduction

"I am conscious of the world through the medium of my body" (1962: 94–95). It is from the body that I perceive the world. Without a body, I have no place from which to perceive the world. "Where is begins with the location of the body. It locates me in a place." [....] "my existence as subjectivity is merely one with my existence as a body and with the existence of the world, and because the subject that I am, when taken concretely, is inseparable from this body and this world". Merleau-Ponty (1962: 408)

In Chapter 1 we outlined the background to the book, and the overall scope of topics to be covered. We address our theme—what is the psychosocial reality of virtual travel?—in stages, waypoints on our journey through the book. To experience any travel phenomena, a person needs to be able to feel they are present in a place. To qualify as travel implies that this place is somewhere other than the person's usual environment. To have the capacity to feel present in this other place, the person must have the prerequisites of feeling they are present somewhere satisfied.

In this chapter we examine what is known about this sense of being somewhere—the experience of *presence in the world*. Arguments are developed from relevant background theories of embodiment, perception, psychology and philosophy. Some of the contemporary philosophical background might be new terrain for the reader, but we feel that it is useful as a grounding to understand our overall argument about the impact of new technologies on the psychosocial realities of experience.

We start by examining philosophical and psychological aspects of perceiving a world from a first-person perspective. Normally, people assume that they perceive the world as it is. This is the layman's perspective on the world. There are exceptions, but in everyday life we normally do not question it—our ordinary conception of perception is of what we experience with our senses. What if the experience is mediated by technology? Can we then still use this common-sense view of perception? Perceptual experience of the environment is complicated, particularly if this involves continuous attention to and active engagement with one's surroundings, and where one's own activities, both physical and attentional, constitute key parts of the experience. One of the motivations for this chapter is to explore the theoretical background for understanding an experience in a virtual environment as an embodied *perceptual experience*.

Guided by our focus on telepresence, we review relevant theories from contemporary philosophy on the nature of perception, as well as discussing dual process theory. Stanovich and West (2000) labelled the two types of cognitive processes System 1 and System 2. Daniel Kahneman made the theory known to a wider audience in his book "Thinking, fast and slow" (2011). He states in his Nobel prize lecture (2002) "judgments and preferences are called 'intuitive' in everyday language if they come to mind quickly and effortlessly, like percepts". Telepresence may rely on rapid and effortless perceptual acceptance, as implied by Lombard and Ditton's (1997) definition of telepresence as "the illusion of non-mediation", along with the idea of *transparency* in the use of technology. We include a consideration of work by Merleau-Ponty on perception, and Heidegger's concepts of technology and transparency. The purpose is to draw attention to theories of relevance to the question: why can we have a telepresence experience—an experience of being there in another place—and how can we account for what it is theoretically?

The Nature of Experiences, and of Experiences of Other Places

Experience is an elusive term, often used without an explanation of what is meant. According to John Dewey (1922, 1925, 1938), experiences arise from the interaction a person has with his or her environment and is a process mediated in a cultural and social context. Experiences are situated; "*In actual experience, there is never any such isolated singular object or event; an object or event is always a special part, phase, or aspect, of an environing experienced world - a situation*". (Dewey, 1938: 67).

Heinemann (1941), with reference to the empiricist school founded by Philinos of Kos in Alexandria, distinguishes between three sorts of experiences. These are: "*immediate experience, mediated experience (that is observation made by others before us), and analogous experience (thus in case of illness which has not been observed it may be useful to compare similar cases)*". Heinemann, in his discussion, refers to J. A. H. Murray (Oxford, 1817) who distinguished between to have an experience of, to learn by experience, and to try something, a tentative experience. Regarding the first of these "*(i) To have, experience of; to meet with; to feel; to suffer; to undergo. We could call this immediate experience; it covers what we immediately feel or undergo during the course of our life*" (Heinemann, 1941: 570).

There is also a cognitive element to experience. Experiences result from knowledge, but experiences also include perceiving through the senses, as well as feeling, and doing. Logue (2009: 9) define perceptual experience as "*experience associated with sense modalities (vision, hearing touch, smell and taste) in virtue of which it appears to one that one's environment is a certain way*". The emphasis is on the word *of*. Therefore, a perceptual experience is a matter of a certain sort of relation between the subject of the experience and what the experience is of, that is the object of the experience. The term "experience" is used in many domains in a more applied manner, directly relevant to our main topic. Researchers such as Gallarza and Gil (2008) observe that "experiences" are a dominant focus of tourism and tourism research. Also, in consumer behaviour studies it is a frequently used term, as in the "experience economy" (Pine II & Gilmore, 1998). In work on the experience economy it is regarded as being a multi-dimensional concept.

In most cases we assume that we perceive the world as it is. This is the layman's perspective on the world. There are exceptions, but in everyday life we normally do not question this—our ordinary conception of perception is what we experience with our senses. Robinson (2012: 618) writes, "*It is, I think, universally agreed that, pre-philosophically, we are all naïve direct realists*". What if the experience is mediated by technology? Should we then use this common-sense view on perception (Hudson, 2012)? Nöe and Thompson (2004: 17) write that perceptual experience is extraordinarily complicated, particularly if one realises that such experience involves a "*temporally extended, active, and attentional encounter with the environment*" where "*the content of experience is brought forth or enacted by this activity*".

The answer we give to this question has implications for the study of digital travel and the telepresence phenomenon. One of the motivations for this research was to explore the theoretical question of how to understand a visual experience in a digital environment (a VR or other kinds of digital media) as a *perceptual experience* (our emphasis).

The Philosophy of Perceptual Experience

The French philosopher René Descartes is often cited in publications on telepresence. Descartes postulated a separation, a dualism, between *res extensa*, (objects located outside the mind) and *res cogitans* (objects located within the mind). This is referred to as the Cartesian view. *Res extensa* is the substance of which the material world is made, while *res cogitans* is the substance of consciousness, the non-material, the thinking entity. According to Descartes *res cogitans* and *res extensa* interact in the brain, and are located in the centre of the brain (Velmans, 1995). Very often the mind–body problem is traced back to René Descartes and many leave out a reference to Galileo Galilei and his influential book *the Assayer* (Galilei, 1623). This is surprising, because in his book Galileo posits a separation between the external world and the mental world, what he calls secondary properties (Manzotti, 2006a). Galileo Galilei published his book 14 years before Descartes' "*Discourse on the Method of Rightly Conducting the Reason, and Seeking Truth in the Sciences*" (1637).

Many have struggled with the mind–body problem (Biocca, 1997). It concerns the relationship between the mind, perceptions and the senses. And why is it a problem? Let us, for a moment, describe telepresence as a conscious state. Then, to use Thomasson's argument "*difficulties arise given the fact that we may have conscious states that present the world as having certain colours, tones, or smells, even when there is no external object possessing these features at all - indeed even when there is no object being perceived*" (Thomasson, 2008: 198). The hard question concerns the relationship that exists between the objective reality of the world around us and the subjective reality of human experience.

The philosopher McGinn (1989) writes that we cannot resolve the mystery of the mind–body problem, the limits of our minds (to understand this) are not the limits of reality and that reality be constrained by what the human mind can conceive. The mind–body problem is not only discussed in philosophy. It is of relevance for cognitive psychology, and all fields that investigate how the mind works and perception. Therefore, the mind–body problem has relevance for how to understand the telepresence phenomenon (Biocca, 1997). This is the backdrop for the first research question: "*Is the telepresence experience, a mediated experience, similar to or different from the perceptual unmediated experience in the material world?*".

Four Philosophical Views on the Nature of Perceptual Experiences

One of our main aims is to better understand the telepresence phenomenon in relation to digital travel experiences. Few will disagree with the statement that a user of a virtual environment has a visual experience *of what is presented* in the VE. Some will argue that, with telepresence, there is only something digital in front of you and not something real. Tim Crane in his discussion about the problems of perception formulates these two questions: "*(i) how should we account for what we see when we see what isn't there? And (ii) how should we account for those properties instantiated in experiences that are not properties of objects of experience?*"

(Crane, 2006: 25). Object of experience refers to what the experience is of, that is physical objects, but also events, olfactory and gustatory experiences (Logue, 2009). Tim Crane is an exponent of the representational view, which many philosophers share (Macpherson, 2014), but there are alternatives such as relationism, enactivism, naïve realism and the sense-data view, which we briefly review in this chapter.

Many telepresence researchers use the word *virtual* as opposite to *real*, but without any discussion of what they mean by real. In our view this is a weakness because it has implications, for instance, for research design. When choosing measurements or observational methods, it is important to keep in mind the differences between these theoretical and ontological views on perception, and whether or not the experience is veridical. In empirical studies, when participants answer survey-questions they have to find the questions and statement meaningful. There is not necessarily a good correspondence between how a layperson uses a term or understands the meaning of a word, and how the researcher or interviewer uses the same term. To ask a participant to explain or distinguish between what is real vs. what is virtual could be distracting or difficult to answer. On the other hand, we would like to know the participant's answer because it may indicate the level of presence that the participant experienced.

The Representational View

In contemporary philosophy there are two common views on perception. The first is the representational or content view. Others, such as Crane (2006) describe this view as intentionalism. Today this is the standard view in philosophy of perception (Egan, 2012); according to Kimble (2014: 2) *"representationalism in one form or another is very influential in philosophical circles today"*. The other common view is relationism.

The representational view is a very popular theory of the nature of experience among philosophers (Macpherson, 2014), but very hard to understand for most readers. Still, we have decided to include the representational view because it gives the most straightforward explanation of telepresence. According to representationalism, what we experience are representations and the representations exist in the brain. For telepresence, this means that the *there* in *being there* is something purely mental.

The following observation by Moore (1903: 25) is well known and often quoted by representationalists. "*When we try to introspect the sensation of blue, all we can see is the blue: the other element is as if it were diaphanous*". Hence, visual experiences are transparent to their subjects.

Some prefer the window or the sheet of glass metaphor to describe experiences. An experience is like a window; you don't look at it, but through it or, according to Michael Tye, visual experience can be characterised as sheets of glass. He writes:

> Peer as hard as you like via introspection, focus your attention in any way you please, and you will only come across surfaces, volumes, films, and their apparent qualities. Visual experiences thus are transparent to their subjects. We are not introspectively aware of our visual experiences any more than we are perceptually aware of transparent sheets of glass. If we try to focus on our experiences, we 'see' right through them to the world outside. (Tye, 2007: 31)

In our view, this window or sheet of glass metaphor can be used to discuss the essence of telepresence and of survey instruments in telepresence that ask about what the visual experience is like.

Many philosophers, psychologists and cognitive scientists talk about perceptual experiences, or perceptual states in general, as representations (Nanay, 2012, 2015). According to representationalism the presentational character of an experience is determined by the representational content it carries; if that representational content concerns external objects and their features, then the presentational character of that experience will involve those objects and features (O'Sulllivan & Shroer, 2012). Therefore, the qualitative character of our sensory experiences, that is, the apparent objects and properties of those experiences, are merely representational. They comprise or contain the content of those experiences without thereby being actually instantiated in the mind (Dretske, 1995; Lycan, 1996; Tye, 1995). Therefore, the representational content of a sensory experience is determined by what it is about; the phenomenal content is determined by what qualitative property it has.

A veridical experience involves two relations to two different sorts of entities: the relation of perceiving to the objects of experience, which are entities like objects, events and the properties of such entities; and the relation of perceptually representing a proposition (Logue, 2009). Philosophers who speak of perception and representation in this way include Burge, Byrne, Chalmers, Crane, Dretske, Harman, Hill, Peacocke, Searle, Siegel and Tye (Dyrstad, 2012).

There are different versions of representationalism. For the question of how to reason about and give explanations for the telepresence experience, the ontological perspective or stance of the author matters. Some advocates of representationalism distinguish between vehicle and content.

Furthermore, the vehicle of representation is *what does the representing* while the content is *what is being represented* or what is supposed to be represented. Vehicle representationalism claims that phenomenal properties are properties of the vehicles of representation rather than properties of the external objects of perception.

> In speaking about representations, then, we must be clear whether we are talking about content or vehicle, about what is represented or the representation itself. It makes a big difference. In the case of mental representations, the vehicle (a belief or an experience) is in the head. Content - what is believed and experienced—is (typically) not. (Dretske, 2003: 68)

Furthermore, experiences and beliefs are conscious, not because you are conscious of them, but because you are *conscious with them* (Dretske, 1993: 281). This is also called a one-level view. Consciousness is fundamentally a matter of awareness of a world and does not require awareness of our own minds, mental states or the phenomenal character of these (Thomasson, 2008).

There is a form of representationalism that can be named indirect realism in which the basic idea is that the brain constructs representations. We perceive appearances, and, in virtue of perceiving these appearances, we perceive the worldly item corresponding to the appearances. Kriegel (2009) holds this view and writes "*perception is mediated in the sense that objective... reality is perceived through, or in virtue of, the perception of something like a realm of appearances*" (Kriegel, 2009: 96).

A representation both brings the mind in perceptual touch with the world and provides the basic form of representation of it, a representation that serves as "input" to belief and knowledge (Dyrstad, 2012). Perceptual states are about something and have a representational (or intentional) content. What a mental state is about is its intentional content or just its content. The content of perception is representational content, where representational content is specified by a representation's accuracy conditions. With this in mind we can ask whether things are as they appear. With telepresence, and, for instance, a VE, we have a digital representation of something that could be purely fantasy, but could also be something that is a quite accurate representation of the material world.

Finally, some have argued that illusions are not a problem for representationalism. The argument is that phenomenal states that are illusory or hallucinatory are like false beliefs.

"*Illusions are a phenomenon easily described within a representational model of perception. Any time our knowledge doesn't accurately model its referent we say things are not as they 'seem' to us"* (Allsop, 2010:199). Locatelli and Wilson (2017) write that:

> (Representational) views have the benefit of unifying a diverse range of experiences, including hallucinations and illusions, with non-perceptual states such as thoughts, beliefs, desires, imaginings, recollections and intentional actions.

Telepresence, feeling present in a distant (or fictional) place, is an experience that some will argue has non-perceptual states. Representationalism is the dominate view in contemporary philosophy and is of value for researchers interested in telepresence theory, but is not often used as a basis for empirical work. However, in philosophy there are alternatives such as relationism, enactivism and the sense-data view.

Relationism

The fundamental idea behind the relational view (also referred to as the object view or the disjunctive view) is that perception makes the world itself manifest to the mind (Crane, 2006). The identity of a visual state is constituted by the physical facts it is about. As Crane puts it: *"in perceptual experience I am not aware of qualities of my experience; I have the experience, and in having the experience, I become aware of the world"* (Crane, 2006: 6). Perception is a direct relation of acquaintance between a subject and an object in the external world. Perceptions are psychologically unmediated in that perceptual contact with the world is achieved through a psychological state that is, in itself, perceptual. Furthermore, *"the qualitative character of experience is constituted by the qualitative character of the scene perceived"* (Campbell, 2002: 114). Snowdon (1980), Putnam (1994), Campbell (2002), Travis (2004), Martin (2004), Brewer (2006), among others, advocate relationism.

McDowell (1994, 2008) is primarily interested in the epistemology of perception. His position—a variety of relationism—is referred to as epistemological disjunctivism. There are two other versions of disjunctivism. They are J. M. Hinton's and Paul Snowdon's experiential disjunctivism, and M. G. F. Martin's phenomenal disjunctivism. (Haddock & Macpherson, 2008). The experiential version is about the nature of experience or more precisely, about perceptual states. Martin (2013) prefers the label evidential disjunctivism. However, according to Locatteli (2016) the term phenomenological disjunctivism is most commonly used.

Often illusions and hallucinations are commented on in discussions of these philosophical standpoints and theories. Soteriou (2010) writes that in a disjunctivist theory of perception, veridical perceptions and hallucinations differ mentally in some significant respect. This is because there are certain mental features that veridical perceptions have that hallucinations cannot have. Disjunctive views analyse visual experience properties in terms of success properties. In the bad cases, the non-veridical cases, they deny that we have the relevant success properties (Pautz, 2010). Brewer (2008: 173) seeks to accommodate illusions inside a relational framework. He argues: "*there can be a 'visually relevant similarity' between a veridical and a non-veridical percept*".

One difference, according to Soteriou (2010) between disjunctivist approaches, is the issue of whether veridical perception should be characterised as involving a relation to *facts* in the subject's environment, or whether veridical perceptions should, rather, be characterised as involving *a relation to* objects, events and their properties. McDowell adopts the former approach, whereas Campbell, Brewer and Martin adopt the latter. Furthermore, Martin argues that a disjunctive naïve realist view is the best error theory concerning perceptual experience and the introspection of experience (Soteriou, 2010).

The ordinary person's view of perception is naïve realism. It can also be named the common-sense view or the default view because it simply endorses the way in which experience subjectively strikes us; we intuitively take our experience to be an experience of worldly objects (Locatelli, 2016). Logue (2009) contends that naïve realism is in the vicinity of relationism. According to Logue (2011: 269): "*Naïve realism…. holds that veridical perceptual experiences fundamentally consist in the subject perceiving physical entities in her environment*". Naïve realists argue that sensory experiences are relations to mind-independent objects (Martin, 2004) and "*Perceiving is …. a matter of the conscious presentation of actual constituents of physical reality themselves*" (Brewer, 2006: 172). Another version of relationism that deserves additional attention is enactivism.

Enactivism

Enactivism (or enactive realism) became known to a wider audience through the book *The Embodied Mind* (Varela et al., 1991). Enactivism holds that perception is the recognition of sensorimotor contingencies, a law-like connection between our actions and resultant sensory input. According to Manzotti (2011) enactivism builds upon the work of other scholars such as Gregory Bateson (1972), James J. Gibson (1972) and Maurice Merleau-Ponty (1962).

Enactive realism is based on two central principles (Roberts, 2012): (1) "*perception consists in perceptually guided action*" and (2) "*cognitive structures emerge from the recurrent sensorimotor patterns that enable action to be perceptually guided*" (Varela et al., 1991: 173). The enactive approach rejects the classical dichotomy between perception and action. The argument is that experiences are inseparable from the perceiver's bodily activities. According to enactivism, perception is not something that passively happens on us, but something we actively do. Furthermore, the human mind is embodied in our entire organism and embedded in the world. With reference to Merleau-Ponty, Varela, Thompsen and Rosch write "*the subject is inseparable from the world, but from a world which the subject itself projects*" (Varela et al., 1991: 4).

How does enactivism view perception? Roberts (2012: 239) writes:

> The enactive realist approach contends...: all perceptual contact, and hence all perceptual consciousness, is critically dependent upon the possession and exercise of cognitive states and abilities. The perceptual relation, on this view, is to be analyzed as a relation of informed, skillful, and active exploration that cannot be instantiated unless the subject of experience is equipped with the right kind of bodily expertise.

The emphasis is on actions and interactions with the environment, and what happens when we act. "*Experience isn't something that happens in us, it is something we do*" (Nöe, 2004: 216). Perception is from this perspective an active exploration of the environment and an interaction with the world. Enactivists argue that the core features of experiential properties are best explained by appeal to specific patterns of sensorimotor activity, through which complex self-organizing systems interact with aspects of their environment (Hutto, 2011). Perceptual presence is the sense we have of the perceptual accessibility via bodily movement (Bower & Gallagher, 2016).

According to Roberts (2012: 240):

> Enactive realism claims that physical entities, scenes, and events bear multiple, objectively-specifiable properties, all of which are possible objects of perception, but not all of which are available to every perceiver. **Perceptual accessibility** (**our** emphasis) is determined not simply by physiology. Visual accessibility is not dependent solely upon the constitution of the

visual system, for example, nor by sensory input, but by what the perceiver knows, which determines what she is able to apprehend in experience.

Therefore, perceptual presence is a matter of access (Nöe, 2008) and we have access to more than what projects on the retina. Perceptual experience is an encounter made possible by our possession and exercise of understanding; it is a *skilled-based access* to what is there.

In support of a sensorimotor approach to perception, Kevin O'Regan (2011) argues that vision is a way of manipulating the environment, an exploratory activity, one motivated and sustained by our interest in our world. Limbeck-Lilienau (2013: 40) write:

> Enactivism is not only a thesis about perceptual content, but also a thesis about the qualitative character of perceptual experience…..The enactive approach conceives perception as an activity, a form of doing or acting, sensorimotor knowledge and practical sensorimotor skills are constitutive for perception.

There has been some discussion of virtual presence by enactivists. For example, to Nöe (2004), virtual content refers to any aspects of objects which are available to perceptual experience without direct, occurrent perception (see also Keefer, 2009). He also discusses virtual presence and states, for example: *"we have the impression that the world is represented in full detail in consciousness because, wherever we look, we encounter detail. All the detail is present, but it is only **present virtually** (our emphasis), for example, in the way that web site's content is present on your desktop"*. (Nöe, 2004: 49)

Telepresence concerns visual experiences. Interaction and action play a key role in this experience. In one of the earliest and most influential papers in telepresence, Steuer's (1992) *Defining Virtual Reality*, the author discusses the two dimensions of telepresence vividness and interactivity. To him these two dimensions constitute the representational powers of the technology.

The Sense-data View

British philosopher George Moore (1903) introduced the sense-data or sense-datum theory, which is also sometimes described as a theory of visual appearance (Snowdon, 2014). When the term sense data was introduced at the beginning of the last century it was a neutral term with regard to the objects of perception. Moore distinguished between the sense datum, which is given to the mind, and the sensation, which is the act or event of being aware of the datum. Furthermore, sense data are mind-dependent, non-physical objects (Price, 1932). The argument is that sense data exist whenever a person perceives anything, by any of the senses, and also whenever a person has an experience qualitatively *like* perceiving, such as a hallucination. Sense data have, according to *Stanford Encyclopedia of Philosophy* (Huemer, 2011), three defining characteristics; (1) sense data are the kind of thing we are directly aware of in perception, (2) sense data are dependent on the mind and 3) sense data have the properties that perceptually appear to us.

The sense-data theory claims that when we have a perceptual experience we are immediately aware of non-physical, mind-dependent objects called sense data, and shares a commitment to the idea that the structure of experience is relational. According to this view there is no mind-independent physical world responsible for the regularity of our perceptual experiences (Foster, 2000, 2008). But *"whenever a sensible quality is present in experience, there must be an object which instantiates this quality"* (Crane, 2005: 253). A sense experience is to be understood as a kind of sensing, where sensing is, or at least affords, awareness of something. When one focuses on one's experience, one *"sees through it"* and becomes aware of a sense datum (Moore, 1903). According to Austin (1962: 2): *"we never directly perceive or sense, material objects or material things, but only sense-data"*. Objects are private mind-dependent entities and sense data are not located in physical space. We see physical things mediated by virtue of seeing real sensory items that we take to correspond to those physical things (Gandarillas, 2011). Sense data are non-physical objects in the mind that we are aware of (Macpherson, 2014).

Sensing is, or at least affords, awareness of something. Moreover, experiences are essentially presentational (Price, 1932). The presentational character of a visual experience is determined not by the external objects/properties that are the subject matter of our perceptual beliefs but by properties of sense data (O'Sullivan & Schroer, 2012). The sense-datum theory takes perceptual consciousness to consist in an awareness of objects, but the objects in question are not the familiar denizens of the physical world, but are instead special, non-physical objects of a markedly peculiar character (Alston, 1999). Awareness of external objects can only be indirect. Item-awareness is a thesis about the objects of experience: whenever one has a visual experience, even if it is hallucinatory, there is something of which one is visually aware (Pautz, 2007). Therefore, there is no appearance-reality distinction.

Sense-datum theorists are indirect realists. According to indirect realism, perception is a triadic relation between perceiver, a physical object that is perceived indirectly, and some private entity that is perceived directly (Brown, 1992). Perceptual access to the external or mind-independent world is indirect, relegated to the knowledge acquired through the representational capacities of sense data (Brown, 2012). Indirect realist can say that sense data are the *medium* by which we perceive the mind-independent world, and no more create a "veil of perception" than the fact that we use words to talk about things creates a veil of words between us and the things we talk about (Crane, 2011). Veil of perception is the idea that all one is immediately aware of is one's perceptual experience of external objects, not the objects themselves. According to Huemer (2011) veil of perception is closely related to skepticism as it empties perception of content. He further states, in a later publication (Huemer, 2011: 1) that:

> Many philosophers have rejected the notion of sense data, either because they believe that perception gives us direct awareness of physical phenomena, rather than mere mental images, or because they believe that the mental phenomena involved in perception do not have the properties that appear to us.

Summary of the Four Theories

The purpose of this review has been to introduce philosophical theories and arguments of relevance to the questions of what are and why do we have telepresence experiences.

Table 2.1 summarises key characteristics of the philosophical theories reviewed above.

On the one hand, it is important to understand that we use words, terms and concepts that come from philosophy. On the other, we might not use (or be able use) the terms in accordance with how they are used in one of these four philosophical theories. Still, in order to reflect on the question of what a telepresence experience is, it is relevant to notice that there are some major differences between these four and how they account for or explain perception, as shown in Table 2.1.

In the next subsection we discuss insights from decision-making and the distinction between a fast, intuitive system and a slower reasoning system. Many choice studies in decision science focus on how we (sometimes) automatically accept information. Insights from these studies can help us to reflect on why we can have telepresence experiences.

Table 2.1 Representationalism, relationism, enactivism and the sense datum theory

	Mediated/unmediated	Perceptual experiences are characterised by:	Explain illusions as:
Represent-ationalism	Perception is mediated	Perceptual experiences consist in representations. Representations locate perceptual states inside the head An experience itself is normally transparent to us while it makes us absorbed in the features of the world it presents. Representation brings the mind in perceptual touch with the world: world <-> representation <-> mind Representationalism denies that we have first-person knowledge of anything except how we are representing the world as being	Normal mis-representations
Relationism	Perception is psychologically unmediated Phrases used: "unmediated openness" "the transparency of experiences"	Perception makes the world itself manifest to the mind. Perception is a direct relation of acquaintance between a subject and an object in the external world. A main idea of a central variant of disjunctivism (relationism) is that perceiving is a direct relation with situations and things	Objects have the power to mislead us, in virtue of their perceptually relevant similarities with other things. Illusions have visually relevant similarities with veridical perceptions

(continued)

Table 2.1 (continued)

	Mediated/ unmediated	Perceptual experiences are characterised by:	Explain illusions as:
Enactivism	Perception is direct. Starting point: (we have an) unmediated relationship with the world	There is a constitutive inter-dependence; perceptual content constitutively depends on law-like relationships between sensory input and motor output. Hence, perceptual experiences are inseparable from the perceiver's bodily activities. Cognition is spanning brain, body and environment	Suggests that illusions are inaccurate or erroneous spatial know-how. Enactivists find non-veridical experiences difficult to explain
Sense datum	Sense data are the medium	Awareness is indirect. Objects are private mind-dependent entities and sense data are not located in the physical space	Visual awareness

Dual Process Theories and Intuitive Judgment

Daniel Kahneman's, 2011 book, *Thinking Fast and Slow*, on the psychology of judgment and decision-making, is highly cited. However, the publications by Evans, Stanovich and West are even more important for the development of the dual process view. It was Stanovich (1999, Stanovich & West, 2000) who first labelled the two types of cognitive processes system 1 and system 2. This was based on Jonathan Evans work in the 1970s and 1980s.

System 1 is rapid, intuitive, automatic and effortless, while system 2 is slow and controlled (Kahneman, 2003). Intuitions can be described as *"thoughts and preferences that come to mind quickly and without much reflection"* (Kahneman, 2002). Although intuitive judgments can be viewed as an extension of perception to judgment, the distinction between perception and judgment is often blurry (Kahneman & Frederick, 2005).

For system 1, the content level is characterised as percepts, something recognised by the senses. Kahneman and Frederick (2002) used the terms intuitive vs. reflective to characterise the two systems. In this research field, there is not an extensive discussion of illusion, but with reference to Gigerenzer (1991) Kahneman and Frederick write *"there is no mystery about the conditions under which illusions appear or disappear: An intuitive judgment will be modified or overridden if System 2 identifies it as biased"*.

Although many researchers know about the theoretical contributions of Sloman (1996), Stanovich (1999), Kahneman and Fredericks (2002) and Kahneman (2002, 2003) on the two modes of thoughts, there is one question that is hard to answer that has to do with the interaction or interplay between the two systems. What is it that can explain or evoke the use of system 2, and the transition between the two systems? Can we control or choose between the two, and how does this relate to the telepresence (and the digital travel) experience?

The Spinozan Model of Rapid Acceptance Response

Dual process theory argues that in system 1 thoughts and preferences come to mind quickly and without reflection. Spinoza suggested that people believe every assertion they understand, but quickly un-believe those assertions that are found to be at odds with other established facts (Gilbert, 1989). Spinoza argued that to comprehend a proposition, a person has to implicitly accept that proposition; only later, if the person realised that this proposition conflicted with some other, might he or she change his or her mind (Gilbert, 1991).

Richter et al. (2009) refer to the notion of an initial acceptance of information as the dual-stage model of comprehension and validation. Few have tried to test the Spinozan belief procedure. However, there are experiments that indicate that people might be able to validate and reject false information early in information processing when they have relevant background knowledge, see Trope and Gaunt (2000), Schul et al., (2004) and Richter et al. (2009).

The following quote from Gerard (1997: 332) summarises the Spinozan Model (see Fig. 2.1): *"perception is quintessentially Spinozan; a percept is immediately believed. Only in the case of rare illusions are our senses tricked into believing what is not there or in to not believing what is there"*. It is a short step from the Spinozan belief procedure to the telepresence experience.

Type 1 processing is a common processing default (Stanovich et al., 2011). A main factor that explains this is the computational ease of system 1. When a user reports "*I had a feeling of being there*", that is in a place in a virtual environment, it might be this fast, automatic system 1 process that contributes to and explains why the user reports that they had the feeling of being there.

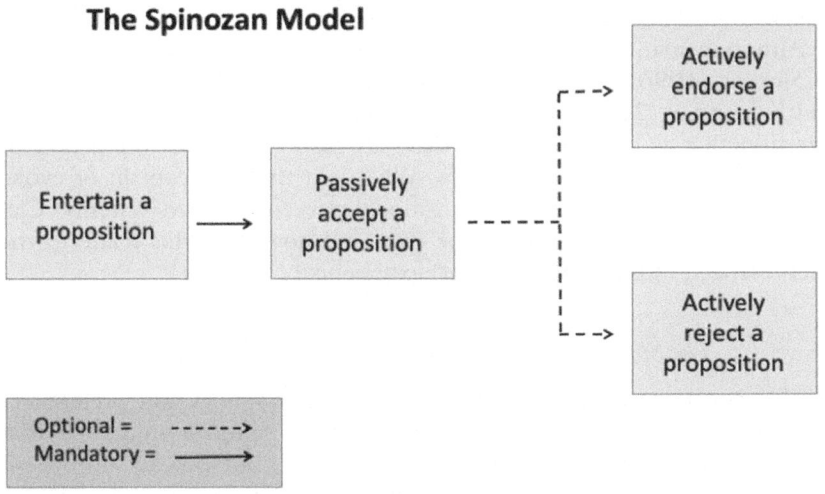

Fig. 2.1 The disposition to accept propositions—The Spinozan model

Table 2.2 Characteristics of System 1 and System 2 thinking

System 1	System 2
Intuitive: Preconscious, automatic and intimately associated with affect	**Rational**: Conscious, deliberative and affect-free
Concrete: Encodes reality in images, metaphors and narratives	**Abstract**: Encodes reality in symbols, words and numbers
Rapid processing: Oriented towards immediate action	**Slower processing**: Capable of long delayed action
Resistant to change: Changes with repetitive or intense experience	**Less resistant to change**: Can change with speed of thought
Integrated: Situationally specific; organised in part by cognitive-affective modules	**Experienced actively and consciously**: We believe we are in control of our thoughts
Self-evidently valid: "Experiencing is believing"	**Not Self-evident:** Requires justification via logic and evidence
Externally focused: Mental presence in the world	**Internally focused:** Mental absence from the world

In discussing the psychology of presence (and telepresence), Waterworth and Riva (2014) characterised the two processes as shown in Table 2.2. According to them, presence can be characterised as the result of intuitive processing.

From judgment and decision theory we now turn to an influential philosopher of the twentieth century, Martin Heidegger. We can ask: how do we interact with and in the world, and what is the role of the body? Heidegger's philosophy of technology, his hammer metaphor and his concepts present-at-hand and ready-to-hand remain important contributions to this discourse.

EVERYDAY ACTIVITIES IN THE WORLD: TRANSPARENCY AND EMBODIMENT

To carry out activities in the world requires embodiment, and is also closely related to the sense of being and of telepresence. Normal, everyday activities need to be, and are, executed frequently and seamlessly. We use our bodies in the world without the need for conscious reflection on how we use them, or even that we are using them. This is one interpretation of the notion of *transparency* in embodiment, and in the use of our bodies and of the tools with which we often carry out our activities in the world.

This notion of transparency can be extended to account for the seamless use of digital systems, and the as-if-unmediated experience of digital media.

Heidegger and Modes of Engaging with the World

Everyday activities are the starting point for Heidegger's philosophy. We have a primary and pragmatic interaction with things and the body plays a central role. To him the world is *at hand* in an almost literal sense. Heidegger (1927) distinguished between a tool being *ready-to-hand* and being *present-at-hand*. His famous example is the hammer which, while in use, is ready-to-hand. It is important to notice that ready-to-hand is not an object of conscious reflection. Packer (1985: 1084) summarises this in the following manner: "*the kind of access of the ready-to-hand mode such as emotions, habitual practices, and skills is radically distinct from the access to phenomena provided by theoretical reflection....* (The ready to hand mode) *is the mode of direct practical engagement in which we actually do much of our everyday living*".

In human–computer interaction (HCI) and usability studies, many researchers cite Heidegger, probably due to this practical interpretation of technology as a tool. Figure 2.2 presents some of Heidegger's concepts with citations that explain the core meaning of the terms.

We can also see Heidegger's concepts as being on different levels of abstraction—see Fig. 2.3. The highest level is the ontological level, the level that incorporates and unifies the lower levels. It is with the concepts on the lower levels that Heidegger explains how we as humans interact, relate to and perceive the world.

Heidegger does not use the term transparency in the specific meaning related to use. For Heidegger *Durchsichtigkeit* has a more general scope than mere contact with technology or tools (Van Den Eede, 2011). To Heidegger circumspection, *Umsicht*, is the skilled possibility of concerned discovering, of concerned seeing. The term denotes the circumstances and the situation of our behaviour and how we understand the world we live in. Herstad (2007: 97) writes: "*Circumspection can be interpreted as a kind of awareness which enables users to see equipment, but without asserting characteristics and properties of the equipment in use, as is the case when an object outside of a use context is seen*". Herstad, therefore, suggests the term *circumspective use* in order to avoid an either/or visible/invisible dichotomy that too often leads to a lack of understanding of the situation

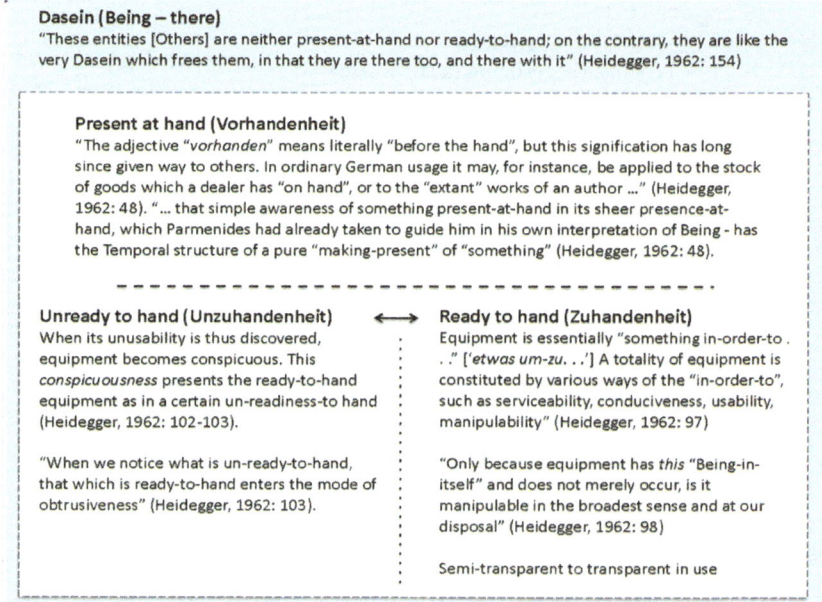

Fig. 2.2 Heidegger and modes of engaging in the world

and context of use. The reason why Heidegger's theory has relevance for VR and telepresence primarily has to do with the transparency or semi-transparency characteristic of the *ready-at-hand* experience.

Researchers in telepresence (e.g. Winograd, 1995; Zahorik & Jension, 1998; etc. Benyon 2012; Sheridan 1999; Turner and Turner (2009, 2012; Turner & Turner 2006)) refer to Heidegger's concepts, but do not discuss *ready-to-hand* in any detail. It is also rare to find researchers that use Heidegger's concepts in empirical studies.

In their paper *Presence as Being-in-the-World*, Zahorik and Jenson (1998) emphasis action as being in the centre of existence. Their thesis is that presence is tied to action in the environment. Söffner (2006: 25) gives credit to Zahorik and Jension in this passage: *"Convincingly in the beginning these authors put forth a definition of presence as 'being-in-the-world'. In introducing Martin Heidegger's thoughts about 'thrownness' (Geworfenheit) and 'readiness-to-hand' (Zuhandenheit) into presence theory, they allow for a distinction between presence as existence in a worldly context defined as state of acting on the one hand, and on*

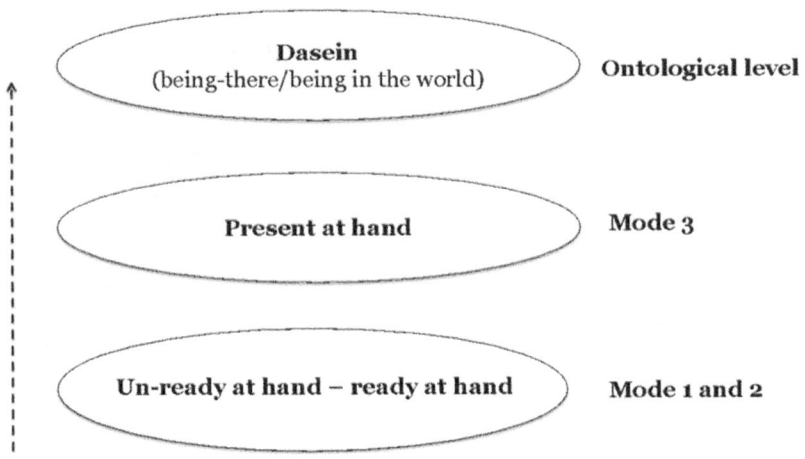

Level of abstraction

Fig. 2.3 Dasein and levels of abstraction

the other interpretation requiring stable (mental) representation that takes place necessarily outside action". Söffner advocates a view similar to Floridi who defines telepresence as an "epistemic failure".

Transparency

Surprisingly, very few authors emphasise the transparency aspect in relation to technologically mediated experiences, although there are exceptions. For instance, Riva (2009: 166) writes: "Following Heidegger, the medium is *ready-to-hand*". When someone has a feeling of being there, the medium is transparent. In her article *The remote body*, Dolezal (2009) discusses telepresence based on ideas and concepts from Husserl, Merleau-Ponty, Sartre and Gallagher. Dolezal (2009: 216) argues: *"The achievement of transparency in the case of manipulating a technological object is of particular interest in the case of telepresence"*.

Don Ihde (2010), a philosopher of science and technology, builds on Heidegger's tool analysis when he discusses transparency. He argues that technology must be transparent enough, not wholly transparent, but *"the closer to invisibility, transparency, and the extension of one's own bodily sense this technology allows, the better"*. (Ihde, 1990: 74).

We can ask: what is it that is transparent? The technology, yes, but not only the technology. Van den Eede (2011: 157) made a summary of philosophical theories discussing the transparency concept and ICT and asserts: *"from a use (or designer's, or engineer's) viewpoint, awareness of the technological mediation must be as low as possible. From a context (or individual's, or reformer's, or victim's) viewpoint, consciousness of it should be as great as can possibly be accomplished. From a theorists' viewpoint, however, some form of double vision should be developed, where both sorts of transparency come in view—otherwise we risk to overlook either one or the other"*.

Some researchers prefer the term visible/invisible to transparency. Weiser (1991) used this as a core concept and to him, the goal is to make ICT-systems objectively visible but subjectively invisible. He states that: *"A good tool is an invisible tool. By invisible, I mean that the tool does not intrude on your consciousness; you focus on the task, not the tool"*. (Weiser, 1994).

EMBODIMENT

We have reviewed enactivism, a theory that puts emphasis on bodily activities. It was influenced by Merleau-Ponty's work as well as Heidegger's. Merleau-Ponty does not explicitly mention Heidegger in his writings, but he has a reference to Heidegger's notion *Dasein* (Matthews, 2002). Merleau-Ponty places the body at the centre of his ontology, the world as we experience it. He writes: *"I am conscious of the world through the medium of my body"* (1962: 94–95). *It is from the body that I perceive the world. Without a body, I have no place from which to perceive the world. 'Where is' begins with the location of the body. It locates me in a place"*. He writes: *"my existence as subjectivity is merely one with my existence as a body and with the existence of the world, and because the subject that I am, when taken concretely, is inseparable from this body and this world"* (Merleau-Ponty, 1962: 408). He uses the term *sentir* to denote a sense experience and the term *coping* to signify how a person is able to respond to particular situations.

By his view, the body is both the generating and the enduring aspect of experience, and an embodied consciousness (Moya, 2014). Merleau-Ponty (1962: 148) writes: *"Our body is not primarily in space, it is of it* and *the body knows how to perceive ... it knows how to act"*. Human subjectivity is essentially an embodied phenomenon, and there is a circular interplay between the three; body–mind–world. For instance, we have learned from our experience how to find our way around in a city. This is *"sedimented in"* how that city looks to us (Dreyfus, 2007: 10). Merleau-Ponty calls this feedback loop between the embodied "coper" and the perceptual world, the intentional arc. He writes: *"Cognitive life, the life of desire or perceptual life – is subtended by an intentional arc which projects round about us our past, our future, (and) our human setting"* (Merleau-Ponty, 1962: 36). Therefore, there is a close connection and an interaction between the human body and the world. According to Fischer and Hencke (1996) Merleau-Ponty might have been influenced by Jean Piaget (1930) who described how we relate to the world as the cycle of action, assimilation and adaptation.

Merleau-Ponty's is also known for the example of the blind man's cane, concerning how we relate to the world. A blind man perceives the world through his cane. This is a skill that has to be learned and is a way of actively probing his environment. When he walks down the street, he is not primarily aware of the cane; instead he is aware of the curb. Like all other perception, it is an active communion with the world. In the context of telepresence and mediated experiences, the screen or the game-console is the cane. The device becomes part of the here-body experience (Ihde, 2002). Likewise, Merleau-Ponty (1962) argues that tools function as an extension of the body. To Merleau-Ponty the body itself is the perceiving subject and *"sight and movement are specific ways of entering into relationship with objects"* (Merleau-Ponty, 1962: 37). Commenting on this statement, Svanaes (2000: 103) writes: *"any theory that locates visual perception in the eyes alone does not do justice to the phenomenon, and that it is meaningless to talk about the perceptual process of seeing without reference to all the senses"*.

To Merleau-Ponty (1962) the most immediate and essential aspects of the lived dimension of space are sensory experiences. In his main work *The Phenomenology of Perception* he reasons as follows: *"by thus remaking contact with the body and with the world we shall rediscover our self, since, perceiving as we do with our body, the body is a natural self and, as it were, the subject of perception"* (Merleau-Ponty, 1962: 239). Nesheim (2011: 29) writes, after reviewing Merleau-Ponty's phenomenology: *"Our bodies are equipped with an extensive set of sensors that allow us to see, smell, hear touch, taste and move in connection with our surrounding"*. Following from this, we consider the senses and their role further below.

Merleau-Ponty's theory of the body is a theory of perception emphasising perceptual awareness (Talero, 2005: 20). To Merleau-Ponty (1962: 229): "*the senses intercommunicate by opening on to the structure of the things*". Therefore, he did not perceive qualities of other parts of perception purely in themselves, but in their integrated relation with other parts (Shores, 2012). In his later writings, Merleau-Ponty reflects on vision and touch. His thesis is that vision, touch and movement are intertwined; we see only what we look at. "*What would vision be without eye movement? And how could the movement of the eyes not blur things if movement were blind? If it were only a reflex?*" Merleau-Ponty (1964: 162). The idea of a touching look should be taken literally. He argues that we should give up the idea of isolating the senses. Vision is intermingled with movement. There is an intrinsic relationship between my body and things around me. Not surprisingly, Merleau-Ponty can be criticised over his views. For instance, he is not consistent in how he uses the term embodiment.

In discussing the blind man's use of a cane (Merleau-Ponty, 1962: 139), he writes that the cane becomes "*incorporated*" into the man's body image (p. 141), but he also writes that the cane becomes "*a bodily auxiliary, an extension of the bodily synthesis*" (p. 153). Although embodiment is emphasised, the body as a unique field of sensory experience is often overlooked in phenomenological investigations influenced by Merleau-Ponty (Leder, 1990). For a further discussion of embodiment and the blind man's cane, see De Preester (2011).

Like "experience", the term "embodiment" is not easy to define. Ziemke (2003) discusses embodiment with the aim of disentangling the different claims and notions about the concept. Although there is disagreement about the meaning (Kiverstein, 2012; Metzinger, 2006) it is a key term for the so-called enactive view (see Sect. "Presence and the Direct Perception Approach"), a view that posits that perception, cognition and action are facets of a single process. As De Vignemont (2011) commented: "*Merleau-Ponty initiated a long tradition of phenomenological investigation of bodilyawareness (Henri* 1965; De Preester, 2007; *Gallagher,* 2005; *Legrand,* 2006; Mishara, 2004; Thompson, 2005; Zahavi & Parnas, 1998), *as well as the recent sensorimotor theories of consciousness* (O'Regan and Noë, 2001; Nöe, 2004; Hurley, 1998; Thompson, 2005)".

In phenomenology and contemporary philosophy, embodiment is a popular term (Gallagher, 2005, 2018; Metzinger, 2004, 2006). Metzinger (2004) connects the concept of presence to that of *transparency*, which refers to the fact that our perceptions of the world and of the self appear direct, unmediated by the neurocognitive mechanisms that in fact give rise to them (Seth et al., 2012). Metzinger further emphasises that what is experienced is experienced now and refers to this as nowness and a temporal window of presence (Wittman, 2011).

Merleau-Ponty's ideas are highly relevant to understanding the phenomena of telepresence. Telepresence is often primarily a visual experience, but not only a visual experience. Other senses need to be invoked and engaged in a virtual environment for a strong sense of *being there* (presence in a digital environment) to be achieved. In the next subsection we discuss work relevant to the question of whether or not our perceptual experiences exist in the brain or outside it, with particular reference to the experience of telepresence.

Presence and the Direct Perception Approach

Loomis asserts that presence is a basic state of consciousness consisting of the attribution of sensation to some distal stimulus or environment. In the inaugural issue of the *Presence: Teleoperators and Virtual Environments* he writes that a simulated environment can "*be so compelling as to force a user to question the assumptions that the physical and perceptual world are one and the same*" (Loomis, 1992: 113). Biocca (2001) suggests, based on a philosophical grounding of a theory of presence, that presence is a sub-problem of the science of consciousness, specifically the mind–body problem. To him VE technologies potentially alter the interaction of the senses and/or motor systems with energy arrays that represent invariants of the environment such as objects, spaces and other beings.

For Biocca, presence is motivated by the desire to transcend the body "*to move beyond the limits of the body and the sensory channels*" (Biocca, 1997: 13) and he calls attention to what he calls the cyborg's dilemma: the extension of the human senses through technology (Mennecke et al., 2010). According to Hillis (1999: 164); "*In VEs, a quasi merger of embodied perception and externally transmitted conception happens at the level of sensation*".

The psychologist Max Velmans (1998, 2009), who advocates a direct perception approach, argues that human experiences occur in the phenomenal realm. Therefore, virtual realities do not fit easily into a world *as-perceived* model: "*that dualists and reductionists assume that experiences either have no location or extension or are located and extended*" (p. 3). In VR one appears to interact with a world outside one's own body although there is no actual and corresponding *there* surrounding the person.

Embodiment provides the necessary bridge between external events and brain events. Sensory and motor apparatuses allow the brain to be part of a causal network linked to the external world (Manzotti, 2006b: 75). According to Velmans (1998, 2009), the VR world appears to have 3D location and extension outside one's body in spite of the fact that it is entirely a phenomenal experience. Therefore, VR does not seem to be without location or extension, or to be in the brain. Perceptual processing in the brain can result in experiences that have a subjective location and extension beyond the brain (Velmans, 1998: 47). Pilotti (2011) argues in a similar manner, he writes: *"it is as self-evident as anything can be that all my sensory experiences are outside the brain, in the body or in the space around me. Touch is in the body where I feel the touch. (and) our sensory experiences are identical with matter, not in the brain, but out there in the now, the space or matter aspect of space–time"* (Pilotti, 2011: 129). To Merleau-Ponty (1962: 169) perception is a continuous interaction involving the subject's intentions, expectations and physical actions.

Mingers (2001), building on Merleau-Ponty, uses the term *embodied cognition* in his works. He argues that information is objective in the sense of being independent of the observer, but the meaning that it generates is observer-dependent. He emphasises the importance of recognising the embodied and situated nature of human cognition and action. The intransitive (ontological) dimension is the domain of the real objects of scientific knowledge; the transitive (epistemological) dimension is the domain of humanly constructed cognitive objective of science such as theories, experiments and concepts. Mingers uses the term structural coupling, a concept that originates from Maturana and Varela's (1980, 1987) and has some similarities with how Merleau-Ponty describes embodiment.

Velmans (2009) writes that in everyday life we take the phenomenal world to be the physical world, and we treat the objects and events we perceive as if they were the objects and events themselves. *"Although we normally think of the phenomenal world surrounding our body as the 'physical world', it remains part of conscious experience rather than apart from it"* (Velmans, 2008: 33).

Velman's point of view is useful since it corresponds to how individuals can experience a VE, and describe their experience when it happens or just after. When someone is sightseeing in a VE of a city that actually exists, it is a predominantly visual experience, but the place is perceived as real (Slater, 1999) or, in telepresence terminology, the person has the feeling of *being there*. How long a feeling of being there lasts varies, and a user of a VE may often have breaks in presence (Slater & Steed, 2000).

Summary and Conclusions

To understand the experience a sense of being in a digital environment—telepresence (or mediated presence—we started this chapter by considering how we can experience being anywhere—our perception of being in the world. We presented different philosophical and psychological perspectives on having the experience of being somewhere, stressing the importance of perception. The motivation for this was to shed light on what possible ways of understanding the experience of being in another world was created or mediated by digital technology.

We compared four philosophical views: representationalism, relationism, enactivism and the sense-data view. Each has its strengths and weaknesses, but relationism is best placed to accommodate perceptual illusions, which is a prevalent view of the psychological nature of telepresence experiences. Enactivism is also very relevant to understanding presence, as it stresses that experiences are inseparable from the perceiver's bodily activities. Each of these approaches has something to offer and add to our understanding of digital travel.

We also introduced dual process theories of cognition and suggested that acceptance of the reality of an external world, in the moment, is largely a result of intuitive, rapid cognitive processing. We emphasised the Spinozan nature of this view, which also suggests that the initial, rapid judgment may be overridden on further reflection, as we discuss in Chapter 3.

Enactivism was heavily influenced by the works of Merleau-Ponty and Gibson, in the light of the relationship between the world, embodiment, action and perception, and how these lead into the concept of transparency in interactions with the world, and with digitally mediated environments. We stressed the importance of Merleau-Ponty's view of how we perceive the world with our bodies. Digitally or not digitally, this is a basic characteristic of human experience.

Direct perception accounts of presence are appealing in the way embodiment is seen as linking mind and body, with perception understood as happening "out there", not in the brain, both for perception of the physical world and of compellingly rendered virtual world. This a key idea for understanding how digital travel can be experienced as perceptually real.

As suggested by enactivism and the direct perception approach, the possibilities for action in the world are important to the nature of our experience of places. This, in turn, is influenced by the characteristics of the world in which we act, through what are known as affordances.

These topics are taken up in Chapters 4 and 5 in the context of digital travel and related experiences of place and telepresence.

A subjective experience of *being there* at a place experienced in the moment can be accounted for theoretically with reference to the theoretical positions reviewed in this chapter. A travel experience—whether physical or digital—will also include the memory of trip, the after-travel experience. When reflecting on a digital travel experience, we will most likely conclude that it was not actual travel. But we can still have a vivid memory of what it was like to be there, if the conditions for successful digital travel have been met.

In the light of the discussions presented in this chapter, the next chapter (Chapter 3) focuses more specifically on views of telepresence, which provide a ground for discussing the related concepts of virtual tourism, place theory and relevant areas of marketing and hedonistic consumption research.

REFERENCES

Allsop, B. (2010). Representational Qualia theory. *Journal of Consciousness Exploration & Research, 1*(2), 193–212.

Alston, W. P. (1999). Back to the theory of appearing. *Nous, 33*(s13), 181–203. https://doi.org/10.1111/0029-4624.33.s13.9

Austin, J. L. (1962). *Sense and sensibilia*. Oxford University Press.

Bateson, G. (1972). *Steps to an ecology of mind: Collected essays in anthropology, psychiatry, evolution, and epistemology*. Ballantine Books.

Benyon, D. (2012). Presence in blended spaces. *Interacting with Computers, 24*(4), 219–226. https://doi.org/10.1016/j.intcom.2012.04.005

Biocca, F. (1997). The Cyborg's dilemma: Progressive embodiment in virtual environments. *Journal of Computer-Mediated Communication, 3*(2). https://doi.org/10.1111/j.1083-6101.1997.tb00070.x

Biocca, F. (2001). Inserting the presence of mind into a philosophy of presence: A response to Sheridan and Mantovani and Riva. *Presence: Teleoperators and Virtual Environments, 10*(5), 546–556. https://doi.org/10.1162/105474601753132722

Bower, M., & Gallagher, S. (2016). Bodily affects as prenoetic elements in enactive perception. *Phenomenology and Mind*, 78–93. https://doi.org/10.13128/PHE_MI-19591

Brewer, B. (2006). Perception and content. *European Journal of Philosophy*, *14*(2), 165–181. https://doi.org/10.1111/j.1468-0378.2006.00220.x

Brewer, B. (2008). How to account for illusion. In A. Haddock & F. Macpherson (Eds.), *Disjunctivism: Perception, action, knowledge* (pp. 168–180). Oxford: Oxford University Press.

Brown, D. H. (2012). Losing grip on the world: From illusion to sense-data. In A. Raftopoulos & P. Machamer (Eds.), *Perception, realism and the problem of reference* (pp. 68–95). Cambridge University Press. https://doi.org/10.1017/CBO9780511979279.004

Brown, H. I. (1992). Direct realism, indirect realism, and epistemology. *Philosophy and Phenomenological Research*, *52*(2), 341. https://doi.org/10.2307/2107939

Campbell, J. (2002). *Reference and consciousness*. Oxford University Press. https://doi.org/10.1093/0199243816.001.0001

Crane, T. (2005). What is the problem of perception? *Synthesis Philosophica*, *20*(2), 237–264.

Crane, T. (2006). Is there a perceptual relation? In S. Gendler & J. Hawthorne (Eds.), *Perceptual experience* (pp. 126–146). Oxford University Press.

Crane, T. (2011). Existence and quantification reconsidered. In T. E. Tahko (Ed.), *Contemporary aristotelian metaphysics* (pp. 44–65). Cambridge University Press. https://doi.org/10.1017/CBO9780511732256.005

De Preester, H. (2007). The deep bodily origins of the subjective perspective: Models and their problems. *Consciousness and Cognition*, *16*(3), 604–618. https://doi.org/10.1016/j.concog.2007.05.002

De Preester, H. (2011). Technology and the body: The (im)possibilities of re-embodiment. *Foundations of Science*, *16*(2–3), 119–137. https://doi.org/10.1007/s10699-010-9188-5

De Vignemont, F. (2011). Bodily awareness: The Standford encyclopedia of phylosophy. In E. Zalta (Ed.), (Fall 2001 ed., Vol. 2012).

Dewey, J. (1922). *Human nature and conduct*. Dover Publications.

Dewey, J. (1925). *Experience and nature*. Dover Publications.

Dewey, J. (1938). *Logic: The theory of inquiry*. Holt.

Dolezal, L. (2009). The remote body: The phenomenology of telepresence and reembodiment. *Human Technology: An Interdisciplinary Journal on Humans in ICT Environments*, *5*(2), 208–226. https://doi.org/10.17011/ht/urn.200911234471

Dretske, F. (1993). Conscious experience. *Mind*, *102*(406), 263–283.

Dretske, F. (1995). *Naturalizing the mind*. MIT Press/Bradford Books.

Dretske, F. (2003). Experience as representations. *Philosophical. Issues*, *13*(September), 67–82.

Dreyfus, H. L. (2007). Why Heideggerian AI failed and how fixing it would require making it more Heideggerian. *Artificial Intelligence, 171*(18), 1137–1160. https://doi.org/10.1016/j.artint.2007.10.012

Dyrstad, J. (2012). *Presence to mind: Representation and perceptual awareness* (Master thesis), Oslo.

Egan, F. (2012). Representationalism. In E. Margolis, R. Samuels & S. Stich (Eds.), *The Oxford handbook of philosophy and cognitive science*. Oxford University Press.

Fischer, K. W., & Hencke, R. W. (1996). Infants' construction of actions in context: Piaget's contribution to research on early development. *Psychological Science, 7*(4), 204–210. https://doi.org/10.1111/j.1467-9280.1996.tb00360.x

Foster, J. (2000). *The nature of perception*. Oxford University Press. https://doi.org/10.1093/0198237693.001.0001

Foster, J. (2008). *A world for us*. Oxford University Press. https://doi.org/10.1093/acprof:oso/9780199297139.001.0001

Galilei, G. (1623). *The Assayer*. Doubleday & Co. https://www.princeton.edu/~hos/h291/assayer.htm

Gallagher, S. (2005). *How the body shapes the mind*. Oxford University Press.

Gallagher, S. (2018). Embodied rationality. In G. Bronner & F. Di Iorio (Eds.), *The mystery of rationality* (pp. 83–94). Springer. https://doi.org/10.1007/978-3-319-94028-1_7

Gallarza, M. G., & Gil, I. (2008). The concept of value and its dimensions: A tool for analysing tourism experiences. *Tourism Review, 63*(3), 4–20. https://doi.org/10.1108/16605370810901553

Gandarillas, F. P. (2011). Sense-data, introspection and the reality of appearances. *Praxis Filosófica, 33*(July/December), 75–105.

Gerard, H. B. (1997). Psychic reality and unconscious belief: A reconsideration. *International Journal of Psychoanalysis, 78*, 327–334.

Gibson, J. J. (1972). A theory of direct visual perception. In J. Royce & W. Rozenboom (Eds.), *The psychology of knowing*. Gordon & Breach.

Gigerenzer, G. (1991). From tools to theories: A heuristic of discovery in cognitive psychology. *Psychological Review, 98*(2), 254–267. https://doi.org/10.1037/0033-295X.98.2.254

Gilbert, D. T. (1989). Thinking lightly about others: Automatic components of the social inference process. In J. S. Uleman & J. A. Bargh (Eds.), *Unintended thought* (pp. 189–211). The Guilford Press.

Gilbert, D. T. (1991). How mental systems believe. *American Psychologist, 46*(2), 107–119. https://doi.org/10.1037/0003-066X.46.2.107

Haddock, A., & Macpherson, F. (2008). *Disjunctivism*. Oxford University Press. https://doi.org/10.1093/acprof:oso/9780199231546.001.0001

Heidegger, M. (1927). *Being and time*. Harper.

Heinemann, F. H. (1941). The analysis of 'experience'. *The Philosophical Review*, 50(6 November), 561–584.
Henri, M. (1965). *Philosophie et Phénoménologie du corps*. Paris: Presses Universitaire de France.
Herstad, J. (2007). *Circumspective use of equipment: The case of bicycle messengers*. Universitetet i Oslo.
Hillis, K. (1999). *Digital sensations: Space, identity and embodiment in virtual reality*. University of Minnesota Press.
Hudson, R. (2012). What is a state of visual perception? *International Journal of Business, Humanities and Technology*, 2(1 January), 130–141. https://doi.org/10.30845/ijbht
Huemer, M. (2011). *Sense data*. Stanford University. plato.stanford.edu.
Hurley, S. (1998). *Consciousness in action*. Cambridge, MA: Harvard University Press.
Hutto, D. (2011). Consciousness. In J. Garvey (Ed.), *The continuum companion to philosophy of mind*. Continuum International Publishing Group.
Ihde, D. (1990). *Technology and the lifeworld: From garden to earth*. Indiana University Press.
Ihde, D. (2002). *Bodies in technologies*. University of Minnesota Press.
Ihde, D. (2010). A phenomenology of technics. In C. Hanks (Ed.), *Technology and values: Essential readings*. Wiley-Blackwell.
Kahneman, D. (2002). *Daniel Kahneman—Prize lecture*. https://www.nobelprize.org/prizes/economic-sciences/2002/kahneman/lecture/
Kahneman, D. (2003). A perspective on judgment and choice: Mapping bounded rationality. *American Psychologist*, 58(9), 697–720. https://doi.org/10.1037/0003-066X.58.9.697
Kahneman, D. (2011). *Thinking, fast and slow*. Farrar.
Kahneman, D., & Frederick, S. (2002). Representativeness revisited: Attribute substitution in intuitive judgment. In T. Gilovich, D. Griffin, & D. Kahneman (Eds.), *Heuristics and biases: The psychology of intuitive judgment* (pp. 49–81). Cambridge University Press. https://doi.org/10.1017/CBO9780511808098.004
Kahneman, D., & Frederick, S. (2005). A model of heuristic judgment. In K. Holyoak & B. Morrison (Eds.), *The Cambridge handbook of thinking and reasoning*. Cambridge University Press.
Keefer, L. A. (2009). *Defending Noe's enactive theory of perception*. Thesis. Georgia State University. https://scholarworks.gsu.edu/philosophy_theses/52
Kimble, K. (2014). Varieties of representationalism and their approach to sensory experience. *Philosophical Papers and Review*, 5(1), 1–12. https://doi.org/10.5897/PPR12.025

Kiverstein, J. (2012). The meaning of embodiment. *Topics in Cognitive Science*, *4*(4), 740–758. https://doi.org/10.1111/j.1756-8765.2012.01219.x

Kriegel, U. (2009). *Subjective consciousness: A self-representational theory*. Oxford University Press.

Leder, D. (1990). *The absent body*. University of Chicago Press.

Legrand, D. (2006). The bodily self: The sensori-motor roots of pre-reflective self-consciousness. *Phenomenology and the Cognitive Sciences*, *5*(1), 89–118. https://doi.org/10.1007/s11097-005-9015-6

Limbeck-Lilienau, C. (2013). *Seeing, blindness and illusion: A defense of the content view in perception*. Universitet Wien.

Locatelli, R. (2016). In Defence of phenomenal disjunctivism. *An Elucidation. Phenomenology and Mind*, *4*, 154–161.

Locatelli, R., & Wilson, K. A. (2017). Introduction: Perception without representation. *Topoi*, *36*(2), 197–212. https://doi.org/10.1007/s11245-017-9460-1

Logue, H. (2009). *Perceptual experience: Relations and representations*. Massachusetts Institute of Technology. http://hdl.handle.net/1721.1/55181

Logue, H. (2011). The skeptic and the naïve realist. *Philosophical Issues*, *21*(1), 268–288. https://doi.org/10.1111/j.1533-6077.2011.00204.x

Lombard, M., & Ditton, T. (1997). At the heart of it all: The concept of presence. *Journal of Computer-Mediated Communication*, *3*(2). https://doi.org/10.1111/j.1083-6101.1997.tb00072.x

Loomis, J. (1992). Distal attribution and presence. *Presence: Teleoperators and virtual environments*. http://dl.acm.org/citation.cfm?id=128955

Lycan, W. G. (1996). *Consciousness and experience*. Bradford Books.

Macpherson, F. (2014). Is the sense-data theory a representationalist theory? *Ratio*, *27*(4), 369–392. https://doi.org/10.1111/rati.12085

Manzotti, R. (2006a). An alternative view of conscious perception. *Journal of Consciousness Studies*, *13*(6), 45–79.

Manzotti, R. (2006b). Consciousness and existence as a process. *Mind and Matter*, *4*(1), 7–43.

Manzotti, R. (2011). *Introduction in situated aesthetics: Art beyond the skin* (R. Manzotti, Ed.). (pp. 1–10). Imprint Academic.

Martin, M. G. F. (2004). The limits of self-awareness. *Philosophical Studies*, *120*(1–3), 37–89. https://doi.org/10.1023/B:PHIL.0000033751.66949.97

Martin, M. G. F. (2013). Shibboleth: Some comments on William Fish's perception, hallucination & illusion. *Philosophical Studies*, *163*(1), 37–48. https://doi.org/10.1007/s11098-012-0075-5

Matthews, E. (2002). *The philosophy of Merleau-Ponty* (1st ed.). Acumen Publishing Limited. https://doi.org/10.1017/UPO9781844653362

Maturana, H. R., & Varela, F. J. (1980). *Autopoiesis and cognition*. Reidel Publishing Company.

Maturana, H. R., & Varela, F. J. (1987). *The tree of knowledge: The biological roots of human understanding*. Shambhala.

McDowell, J. (1994). Mind and world. *Philosophical Books, 38*(3), 169–181. https://doi.org/10.1111/1468-0149.00066

McDowell, J. (2008). The disjunctive conception of experience as material for a transcendental argument. In A. Haddock & F. Macpherson (Eds.), *Disjunctivism: Perception, action, knowledge* (pp. 376–389). Oxford University Press.

McGinn, C. (1989). Can we solve the mind—Body problem? *Mind, 98*(391), 349–366.

Mennecke, B. E., Triplett, J. L., Hassall, L. M., & Conde, Z. J. (2010). Embodied Social presence theory. *2010 43rd Hawaii International Conference on System Sciences* (pp. 1–10). https://doi.org/10.1109/HICSS.2010.179

Merleau-Ponty, M. (1962). *Phenomenology of perception* (1962 (Paris: Gallimard, 1945)). Routledge and Kegan Paul.

Merleau-Ponty, M. (1964). Eye and mind. In *The primacy of perception: And other essays on phenomenological psychology, the philosophy of art, history, and politics*. Northwestern University Press.

Metzinger, T. (2004). *Being no one*. MIT Press.

Metzinger, T. (2006). Reply to Gallagher: Different conceptions of embodiment. *PSYCHE: An Interdisciplinary Journal of Research On Consciousness, 12*(4), 1–7.

Mingers, J. (2001). Embodying information systems: The contribution of phenomenology. *Information and Organization, 11*(2), 103–128. https://doi.org/10.1016/S1471-7727(00)00005-1

Mishara, A. L. (2004). The disconnection of external and internal in the conscious experience of schizophrenia: Phenomenological, literary and neuroanatomical archaeologies of self. *Philosophica, 73*, 87–126.

Moore, G. E. (1903). The refutation of idealism. *Mind, 12*(48), 433–453.

Moya, P. (2014). Habit and embodiment in Merleau-Ponty. *Frontiers in Human Neuroscience, 8*. https://doi.org/10.3389/fnhum.2014.00542

Nanay, B. (2012). Empirical problems with anti-representationalism. In B. Brogaard (Ed.), *Does perception have content?* (pp. 39–50). Oxford University Press.

Nanay, B. (2015). The representationalism versus relationism debate: Explanatory contextualism about perception. *European Journal of Philosophy, 23*(2), 321–336.

Nesheim, E. (2011). *Framing embodiment in general-purpose computing: A study identifying key components in a multimodal general-purpose computational environment* [Universitet i Bergen]. https://bora.uib.no/bora-xmlui/handle/1956/6310

Nöe, A. (2004). *Action in perception*. MIT Press.

Nöe, A. (2008). Reply to Campbell Martin and Kelly. *Philosophy and Phenomenological Research, 76*(3), 691–706.

Nöe, A., & Thompson, E. (2004). Are there neural correlates of consciousness? *11*(1), 3–28.

O'Regan, J. K. (2011). *Why red doesn't sound like a bell*. Oxford University Press. https://doi.org/10.1093/acprof:oso/9780199775224.001.0001

O'Regan, J. K. & Noë, A. (2001). A sensorimotor account of vision and visual consciousness. *Behavioral and Brain Sciences, 24*(5), 939–973. https://doi.org/10.1017/S0140525X01000115

O'Sullivan, B., & Schroer, R. (2012). Painful reasons: Representationalism as a theory of pain. *The Philosophical Quarterly, 62*(249), 737–758. https://doi.org/10.1111/j.1467-9213.2012.00092.x

Packer, M. J. (1985). Hermeneutic inquiry in the study of human conduct. *American Psychologist, 40*(10), 1081–1093. https://doi.org/10.1037/0003-066X.40.10.1081

Pautz, A. (2007). Intentionalism and perceptual presence. *Philosophical Perspectives, 21*(1), 495–541. https://doi.org/10.1111/j.1520-8583.2007.00134.x

Pautz, A. (2010). Why explain visual experience in terms of content. In *Perceiving the world* (B. Nanay, ed.) (pp. 254–309).

Piaget, J. (1930). *The Child's conception of physical causality*. Harcourt.

Pilotti, J. (2011). Consciousness and physics: Towards a scientific proof that consciousness. *Journal of Transpersonal Research, 3*, 123–134.

Pine II, J. B., & Gilmore, J. H. (1998, July–August). Welcome to the experience economy. *Harvard Business Review*.

Price, H. H. (1932). *Perception*. Methuen & Co.

Putnam, H. (1994). Sense, nonsense, and the senses: An inquiry into the powers of the human mind. *The Journal of Philosophy, 91*(9), 445. https://doi.org/10.2307/2940978

Richter, T., Schroeder, S., & Wöhrmann, B. (2009). You don't have to believe everything you read: Background knowledge permits fast and efficient validation of information. *Journal of Personality and Social Psychology, 96*(3), 538–558. https://doi.org/10.1037/a0014038

Riva, G. (2009). Is presence a technology issue? Some insights from cognitive sciences. *Virtual Reality, 13*(3), 159–169. https://doi.org/10.1007/s10055-009-0121-6

Roberts, T. (2012). Exploring enactive realism. *International Journal of Philosophical Studies, 20*(2), 239–254. https://doi.org/10.1080/09672559.2011.629671

Robinson, H. (2012). Relationalism versus representationalism: How deep is the divide? *The Philosophical Quarterly, 62*(248), 614–619. https://doi.org/10.1111/j.1467-9213.2012.00060.x

Schul, Y., Mayo, R., & Burnstein, E. (2004). Encoding under trust and distrust: The spontaneous activation of incongruent cognitions. *Journal of Personality and Social Psychology*, *86*(5), 668–679.

Seth, A. K., Suzuki, K., & Critchley, H. D. (2012). An interoceptive predictive coding model of conscious presence. *Frontiers in Psychology*, 2. https://doi.org/10.3389/fpsyg.2011.00395

Sheridan, T. B. (1999). Descartes, Heidegger, Gibson, and god: Toward an eclectic ontology of presence. *Presence: Teleoperators and Virtual Environments*, *8*(5), 551–559. https://doi.org/10.1162/105474699566468

Shores, C. (2012). Body and world in Merleau-Ponty and Deleuze. *Studia Phaenomenologica, Romanian Society for Phenomenology*, *12*, 181–209. https://doi.org/10.7761/SP.12.181

Slater, M. (1999). Measuring presence: A response to the Witmer and Singer presence questionnaire. *Presence: Teleoperators and Virtual Environments*, *8*(5), 560–565. https://doi.org/10.1162/105474699566477

Slater, M., & Steed, A. (2000). A virtual presence counter. *Presence: Teleoperators and Virtual Environments*, *9*(5), 413–434. https://doi.org/10.1162/105474600566925

Sloman, S. A. (1996). The empirical case for two systems of reasoning. *Psychological Bulletin*, *119*(1), 3–22. https://doi.org/10.1037/0033-2909.119.1.3

Snowdon, P. (1980). Perception, vision and causation. *Proceedings of the Aristotelian Society, New Series*, *81*(1980–1981), 175–192.

Snowdon, P. (2014). The philosophy of perception: An introduction. In B. Dainton & H. Robinson (Eds.), *The Bloomsbury companion to analytic philosophy* (pp. 453–473). Bloomsbury Publishing.

Söffner, J. (2006). What production of presence and Mimesis have in common. *Proceedings of the 9th International Workshop on Presence*.

Soteriou, M. (2010). The disjunctive theory of perception. In E. Zalta (Ed.), *Stanford encyclopedia of philosophy*. Stanford University.

Stanovich, K. E., & West, R. F. (2000). Individual differences in reasoning: Implications for the rationality debate? *Behavioral and Brain Sciences*, *23*(5), 645–665. https://doi.org/10.1017/S0140525X00003435

Stanovich, K. F. (1999). *Who is rational? Studies of individual differences in reasoning*. Lawrence Erlbaum Associates Publishers.

Stanovich, K. E., West, R. F., & Toplak, M. E. (2011). Individual differences in essential components of heuristics and biases research. In K. Manktelow, D. Over & S. Elqayam (Eds.), *The science of reason: A festschrift for Jonathan St BT Evans*. Psychology Press.

Steuer, J. (1992). Defining virtual reality: Dimensions determining telepresence. *Journal of Communication*, *42*(4), 73–93. https://doi.org/10.1111/j.1460-2466.1992.tb00812.x

Svaneas, D. (2000). *Understanding interactivity: Steps to a phenomenology of human-computer interaction*. Norges teknisk-naturvitenskapelige universitet.

Talero, M. (2005). Perception, normativity, and selfhood in Merleau-Ponty: The spatial 'level' and existential Space. *The Southern Journal of Philosophy, 43*(3), 443–461. https://doi.org/10.1111/j.2041-6962.2005.tb01962.x

Thomasson, A. L. (2008). Phenomenal consciousness and the phenomenal world. *The Monist, 91*(2), 191–214.

Thompson, E. (2005). Sensorimotor subjectivity and the enactive approach to experience. *Phenomenology and the Cognitive Sciences, 4*(4), 407–427. https://doi.org/10.1007/s11097-005-9003-x

Travis, C. (2004). The silence of the senses. *Mind, 113*(449), 57–94. https://doi.org/10.1093/mind/113.449.57

Trope, Y., & Gaunt, R. (2000). Processing alternative explanations of behavior: Correction or integration? *Journal of Personality and Social Psychology, 79*(3), 344–354. https://doi.org/10.1037/0022-3514.79.3.344

Turner, P. (2012). An everyday account of witnessing. *AI & Societty, 27*(1), 5–12. https://doi.org/10.1007/s00146-011-0323-9

Turner, P., & Turner, S. (2006). Place, sense of place, and presence. *Presence: Teleoperators and Virtual Environments, 15*(2), 204–217. https://doi.org/10.1162/pres.2006.15.2.204

Turner, P., & Turner, S. (2009). Triangulation in practice. *Virtual Reality, 13*(3), 171–181. https://doi.org/10.1007/s10055-009-0117-2

Tye, M. (1995). *Ten problems of consciousness: A representational theory of the phenomenal mind*. MIT Press.

Tye, M. (2007). Philosophical problems of consciousness. In M. Velmans & S. Schneider (Eds.), *The Blackwell companion to consciousness* (pp. 23–35). Wiley-Blackwell.

Van Den Eede, Y. (2011). In between us: On the transparency and opacity of technological mediation. *Foundations of Science, 16*(2–3), 139–159. https://doi.org/10.1007/s10699-010-9190-y

Varela, F. J., Rosch, E., & Thompson, E. (1991). The embodied mind: Cognitive science and human experience. *The MIT Press*. https://doi.org/10.7551/mitpress/6730.001.0001

Velmans, M. (1995). The relation of consciousness to the material world. *Journal of Consciousness Studies, 2*(3), 255–265.

Velmans, M. (1998). Physical, psychological and virtual realities. In John Wood (Ed.), *The virtual embodied: Presence, practice, technology*. Routledge.

Velmans, M. (2008). Reflexive monism. *Journal of Consciousness Studies, 15*(2), 5–50.

Velmans, M. (2009). *Understanding consciousness*. Routledge. https://doi.org/10.4324/9780203882726

Waterworth, J. A., & Riva, G. (2014). *Feeling present in the physical world and in computer-mediated environments*. Palgrave Macmillan.

Weiser, M. (1991). The computer for the 21st century. *Scientific American*, 265(3), 94–104. https://doi.org/10.1038/scientificamerican0991-94

Weiser, M. (1994). Creating the invisible interface: (Invited talk). *Proceedings of the 7th Annual ACM Symposium on User Interface Software and Technology - UIST '94*, 1. https://doi.org/10.1145/192426.192428

Winograd, T. (1995). Heidegger and the design of computer systems. In A. Feenberg & A. Hannay (Eds.), *Technology and the politics of knowledge* Indiana University Press.

Wittmann, M. (2011). Moments in time. *Frontiers in Integrative Neuroscience*, 5. https://doi.org/10.3389/fnint.2011.00066

Zahavi, D., & Parnas, J. (1998). Phenomenal consciousness and self-awareness: A phenomenological critique of representational theory. *Journal of Consciousness Studies*, 5(5–6), 687–705.

Zahorik, P., & Jenison, R. L. (1998). Presence as being-in-the-world. *Presence: Teleoperators and Virtual Environments*, 7(1), 78–89. https://doi.org/10.1162/105474698565541

Ziemke, T. (2003). What's that thing called embodiment? *Avant: Trends in Interdisciplinary Studies*, 6(2–3), 161–174.

Open Access This chapter is licensed under the terms of the Creative Commons Attribution 4.0 International License (http://creativecommons.org/licenses/by/4.0/), which permits use, sharing, adaptation, distribution and reproduction in any medium or format, as long as you give appropriate credit to the original author(s) and the source, provide a link to the Creative Commons license and indicate if changes were made.

The images or other third party material in this chapter are included in the chapter's Creative Commons license, unless indicated otherwise in a credit line to the material. If material is not included in the chapter's Creative Commons license and your intended use is not permitted by statutory regulation or exceeds the permitted use, you will need to obtain permission directly from the copyright holder.

CHAPTER 3

Feeling Present in Virtual Environments

Abstract We compare and contrast different current theoretical accounts of telepresence, including presence as a pretence (a simulation of reality), as pretending (making believe the virtual world is real), as a perceptual illusion ("the illusion of non-mediation"), and as embodied attention to the surrounding (or apparently surrounding) environment. These views are well-accepted in the field, and can be seen as contributing to a virtual travel experience, which is a kind of illusion. When we feel highly present, we believe in the perceived world in which we experience ourselves to be—it is in that moment real to us. Creating that effect is a key part of a convincing digital travel experience. To have that experience, we must be attending to the digital world, feeling as if we are physically surrounded by it. Our imaginations are involved in how we perceive our surroundings, and in how we conceptualise being there.

Keywords Telepresence · Illusions · Attention · Pretence · Pretending · Imagination

INTRODUCTION

In Chapter 2 we reviewed perspectives on how we can perceive ourselves to be present in the world. For digital travel to be possible, it is necessary to feel present in another place. That is, to feel present in a different place, real or fictional, that is not the place in which the observer is physically located. This is a place that is perceived as being present but is a product of, or in some way mediated by, digital technology. In this chapter the main focus is on this experience of being present in another place, experienced *presence*, particularly through the medium of interactive technologies, which is termed *telepresence* or *mediated presence* (we use these two terms synonymously). We see presence—the sense of being present—as a general human faculty to experience being somewhere, in a particular place, and telepresence as presence elicited via digital technology. We explore several different views on the nature of presence and telepresence, and the factors that may affect the digital traveller's experience of apparently being in another place, one that he is visiting.

First, we can raise the question: what's the main difference between physical travel and digital travel? In both, the pre-departure stage of any journey might be very similar, and most likely mediated by digital technology; searching for places to visit, things to see and so on. And after the event, recollecting, looking at images, telling people about memories of the trip are also quite similar—and in both cases is likely to be at least partly digitally mediated. The story or narrative through which the traveller plans and makes sense of the journey may be very similar in many respects. What is most obviously different between the two is that with digital travel, the traveller's body can be seen as being left behind. The body is located in a different place from the destination in which the traveller feels herself to be—it remains at home.

Digital travel is an experience of being *at a distance* (from the place the body is actually located) a form of telepresence or mediated presence. It feels as if the body, by virtue of which the perceiver experiences the world, travels. But, in actuality, the physical body remains at home. Telepresence is thus a paradoxical state for the perceiver. The word has two parts. *Tele* is the Greek word for *at a distance* and *presence* is about the subjective *here and now* experience. Sometimes the word *presence* is used as a short form of *telepresence*, sometimes to refer more generally to the subjective *here and now* experience. Telepresence implies the use of technology, and is sometimes referred to as *mediated, computer-mediated* or *technology-mediated presence*.

During the last three decades, many researchers have been interested in telepresence. This is partly due to technological developments, in particular the gaming technology and the role that games play in our society. In computer games there has been significant technological advancement in recent years, in particular in photo-realistic computer graphics. As a result, interactive technology can be used to create virtual environments that look very much like the external world in which we live; in fact, we might not always be able to see the difference. Social presence refers to the salience of people other than the observer in an interaction in a virtual environment and is an important aspect of being in a place. For example, tourists do not only have a spatial experience of place with buildings, nature and attractions—they meet other visitors and residents. Tourists also interact in host–guest relations; that is, with employees of hospitality and tourism facilities, and other people that they meet there.

A video game context can enable the perception of action in another place when watching images on a screen while sitting in a chair. Another example might be a website for a destination developed for marketing purposes. In this marketing context we can ask: what is the effect of this website on the user? An interview may reveal that one user of the website just considers the portrayed destination to be beautiful, while another person who looks at the same website decides it is time to book accommodation, find out how to get there and search for events and what to do upon arrival. The second example corresponds to the notion of perceptible affordance that we revisit later. The question is: How do we operationalise affordance in this kind of context? We return to this question in Chapter 5, where we present empirical findings related to virtual tourism.

The origin of the term "virtual reality" can be traced back to Antonin Artaud and his seminal book *The Theatre and Its Double* (1938), Artaud described theatre as "*la réalité virtuelle*", a virtual reality "*in which characters, objects, and images take on the phantasmagoric force of alchemy's visionary internal dramas*". It has become common to see the two words virtual and real in the same sentence. Often the message is that Virtual Reality (VR) is different from real or it is the opposite of real. In most cases there is no discussion on what it is meant by real.

Schloerb (1995) proposed that perfect telepresence occurs when the observer cannot discriminate virtual from "actual". Deleuze (1994: 208) writes *"the virtual is opposed not to the real but to the actual"*. The computer graphics could be accurate; that is, what the person sees corresponds to how the place is in the material world when one visits the place. Still, some will argue that it is computer graphics or VR and therefore not real. Schloerb (1995) and then Lee (2004) suggest that sometimes it is more appropriate to use the term actual instead of real. Another term that can be used is face-to-face. This indicates that there is no technology involved; no screen, images or communication through a medium. To Schudson (1978) the unmediated conversation is the ideal fully interactive experience. In many cases *face-to-face* may be an even more fitting term than *actual* or *real*. In particular this is appropriate when we use ordinary language (Etzioni & Etzioni, 1999).

Some installations or apparatus can be regarded as forerunners of today's VR-technology, and were made to create a telepresence experience. In 1420 the Venetian engineer Giovanni Fontana designed *castellum umbrarum*, a castle of shadows (see Fig. 3.1).

Codognet (2003) describes this apparatus as a pre-cave installation and probably one of the first known examples of VR. It has a room with walls composed of folded screens and lighted from behind. What the person in the room sees is moving images that convey a sense of being in a different place.

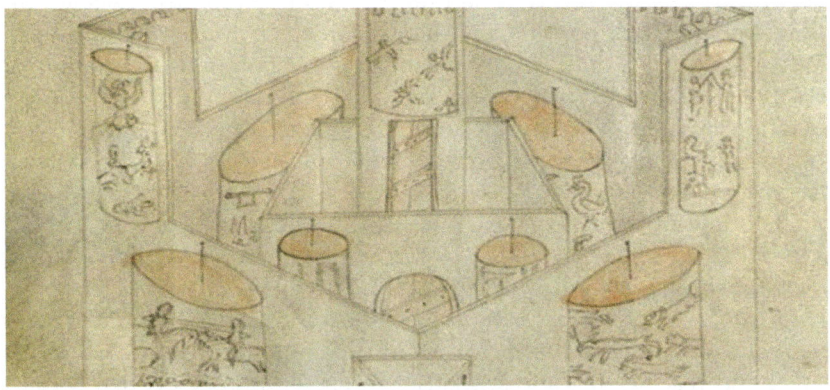

Fig. 3.1 A section of Castellum umbrarum (Giovanni Fontana, 1420, Bayerische Staatsbibliothek)

Today the term telepresence is used to describe the use of technology that allows a person to feel as if he or she is present at a place other than the physical location. According to Marvin Minsky (1980), Patrick Gunkel coined the term in 1979 to refer to tele-operation technology that provides the user with a remote presence in a different physical location via displays and feedback systems. But the concept of telepresence is actually older and more general, referring to a feeling of presence via any kind of digital medium, but did not emerge as a research field until the 1990s.

Conceptualisations of Telepresence: Being Present at a Distance

In this section, we focus on a few different views of telepresence, which can help in furthering our understanding of the nature of digital travel.

The Illusion *of non-Mediation*

Perhaps the most highly cited definition of presence is by Lombard and Ditton (1997). They conceptualise telepresence as a kind of illusion, the perceptual illusion of non-mediation. This implies that they regard telepresence as a property of a person. It results from an interaction between formal and content characteristics of a medium and characteristics of the media user, and therefore it can and does vary across individuals and across time for the same individual. However, they do not explain or discuss the use of the term "illusion", which can have more than one interpretation. In the same vein, to Riva (1999: 91) "*the key issue for developing satisfying virtual environments is measuring the **disappearance of mediation** (*our emphasis*), a level of experience where the VR system and the physical environment disappear from the user's phenomenal awareness*".

This is an almost ubiquitous and very influential view of presence, resonating with the blind man's cane example of Merleau-Ponty (1962) and the notion of transparency discussed in Chapter 2. The blind man walks down the street, exploring the world with his cane. He is not primarily aware of the cane, but of what he perceives with its active use. In the context of telepresence and mediated presence, the medium (the display and the input devices) correspond to the cane. The VR technology disappears for the perceiver, and becomes part of the here-body experience (Ihde, 2002).

Lombard and Ditton's (1997) description of presence is appealing and well-accepted, but has some limitations. It is essentially a formulation of presence as "being there", at least perceptually. We perceive we are in a place without being distracted by the mediating technology, which has become transparent. But is this sufficient for the presence experience? Is it an illusion, or simply that the perceiver doesn´t notice the medium?

Pretending the Digital Is Physical

Turner and his colleagues have argued for the importance *believing* has for real-world presence but for the importance of *pretending* (to believe) or make-believing, for computer-mediated presence. For example, Turner et al. (2014: 1) suggest that: "*A principal, but largely unexplored, use of our cognition when using interacting technology involves pretending. To pretend is to believe that which is not the case, for example, when we use the desktop on our personal computer we are pretending, that is, we are pretending that the screen is a desktop upon which windows reside. But, of course, the screen really isn't a desktop*".

Turner et al. (2014) states that when we play a computer game "*we temporarily believe that we are killing aliens*". He suggests that at some reflective level we know we are not killing aliens, but we have the vivid experience that we are, thanks to the game technology and media content. This seems to be another formulation of presence seen as the experiential illusion of non-mediation, but is not what is commonly understood by *pretending*. On the contrary, pretending seems to be characterised by *not* believing, not by the temporary belief that a mediated experience is real.

While belief does seem to play a role in presence for both the physical world and computer-mediated environment, we suggest it is not a prerequisite, but a consequence, of presence. The old saying "seeing is believing" can be rephrased as *presence is believing*. Following Spinoza, as discussed in Chapter 2, we can say that when we feel present in a world, it *is* real for us in that moment. We believe it to be the case in the here and now of experience, without pretending to.

When we feel presence, we may know (at some level) that the experience is not based on the body being where it is felt to be, but we do not need to pretend to experience this as real. But people vary in terms of how willing they are to have this experience in a digital environment. User characteristics, such as expressed willingness to experience presence in a

VE, affect the level of presence reported (e.g. Cummings & Bailenson, 2016; Sas & O'Hare, 2003).

Turner et al. (2014) argues for presence as make-believe from a type-2 cognitive process point of view (see our discussion of dual process theory in Chapter 2), the result of relatively slow and deliberative thinking. But this contradicts the idea that presence arises in situations where fast and instinctive bodily responses (from a type-1 cognitive process) are called for, for example, in a fast-paced computer game. As Waterworth and Riva (2014: 38) describe presence as "the sheer subjective experience of being in a given environment (the feeling of 'being there') that is the product of an intuitive experience-based metacognitive judgment".

Experiencing a Convincing Simulated Semblance (of Physical Reality)

By this view, presence in a VR results when the simulation elicits similar reactions in an observer to the corresponding place in the physical world (Slater, 2003). Presence is "the total response to being in a place, and to being in a place with other people". (Slater, 2002, p. 7). Slater (2009) suggests that presence in VR is "the extent to which people respond realistically within a virtual environment, where response is taken at every level from low-level physiological to high-level emotional and behavioural responses" (p. 3555). Slater further suggests that this depends on two illusions, the "place illusion" (PI) and the "plausibility illusion" (Psi). He says that: "If you are there (PI) and what appears to be happening is really happening (Psi), then this is happening to you! Hence you are likely to respond as if it were real" (p. 3555). The key phrase here is "is really happening".

One is unlikely to feel much presence in a poorly rendered VR, a low-quality simulation of reality, with unrealistic sound and a perceptible lag between actions and the corresponding events in the virtual world. In the physical world, the form is to a large extent given, and things behave and respond according to our embodied and largely unconscious expectations. Any measure of presence in a VR is only useful, according to this approach, when compared to results of the same measure taken in a physical situation. The more similar the reaction in the VR is to that in the physical world, the greater the degree of presence.

But if presence is the total response to a simulation, as compared to the total response to the physical environment being simulated, how do we assess presence in virtual environments that convey fictional realities?

If no comparison with reality is involved, how can the "total response" be quantified? This view suggests that presence is the degree of similarity with physical reality, not a basic state of consciousness.

It seems reasonable that if the form of the physical world can be accurately simulated, we will have the same experiences in the mediated world as in the physical one. And we will have the same level of presence. But that does not imply that the level of presence experienced in a virtual environment is the same as the level of accuracy of the simulation, as how well the semblance is executed. We can sometimes feel little presence in the physical world—during a boring lecture, for example. If we accurately simulate that experience in a virtual environment we will also feel little presence. Therefore, presence cannot be purely a matter of experiencing a realistic semblance of a place. But is it *an illusion*?

Telepresence and Perceptual Illusions

Many accounts of presence see it as resulting from some form of illusion. The concept of illusion is closely related to that of belief. To the best of our knowledge, Turner is the only theorist to discuss belief, which we see this as another key concept for a more general understanding of the characteristics of presence.

There are a number of different accounts of perceptual illusions. The psychologist Osvaldo Da Pos (1996, 1997, 2008) distinguished between the two kinds. The first are the psychophysical illusions that are discrepancies between what we perceive, for example, redness, and the physical, not perceivable variables, for example, wavelength, which are known to be correlated (Da Pos, 1997: 37). The second are the phenomenological illusions. These are discrepancies within the phenomenal world. When these occur, the same perceived object appears at one time with some characteristics and at another time with different characteristics.

According to Reynolds (1988) the psychological concept of illusion can be defined as a process involving an interaction of logical and empirical considerations. Common usage suggests that an illusion is a discrepancy between one's awareness and some stimulus. (Reynolds, 1988) After proposing and rejecting five definitions of illusion based on this usage, he redefines illusion without reference to truth or falsity, as: *"a discrepancy between one's perceptions of an object or event observed under different conditions"* (Reynolds, 1988: 217).

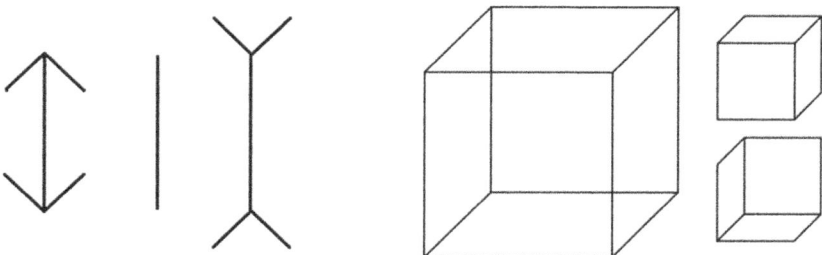

Fig. 3.2 The Müller-Lyer illusion and the Necker cube

Byrne (2009) argued that there is no direct path from the persistence of illusion to the belief-independence of experience. To him, the Müller-Lyer illusion (see Fig. 3.2) involves a belief that one line is longer than the other, and another, more reflective belief that they are of the same length. This is relevant to the way presence may work; we may know, reflectively, that what we experience in a VR is not really happening, but our experience is that it is and, in the moment of experiencing, we may actually believe that it is happening.

Turner et al. (e.g. 2016) makes the same point, although they equate mediated presence with make-believing, with pretending to believe, rather than *actually* believing—which reduces the coherence of his position, unless we are pretending to experience an illusion. Turner and colleagues state that make-believe "is a form of cognition which is decoupled from the real world and which enables us to explore and engage with fictional or imaginary worlds" (Turner et al., 2014).

Voss et al. (2011) posit the notion of the spectator as surrogate body. The word *Leihkörper* literally means "*loan body*". This concept emphasises the basic structure of the illusion that informs the cinematic experience. Voss et al. argue that cinema is an *illusion-forming medium* and that cinematic illusion emerges from the spectator's engagement with the virtual or loan body of the film. Their thesis is that it is "only the spectator's body, in its mental and sensorial-affective resonance with the events on-screen, which 'loans' a three-dimensional body to the screen and thus flips the second dimension of the film event over into the third dimension of the sensing body" (2011: 145). Voss and her colleagues build on Michael Polanyi's (1966) work on the tacit dimension.

As an example of a perceptual illusion, imagine that you are out late at night, walking alone, taking a short-cut to get home. It is dark and there seems to be no-one else around. Your walk takes you through a particularly secluded area, perhaps a path through some woods, across a park, or down dark and deserted streets. You wanted to get home quickly, so you chose this route. But now you start to feel afraid. You see what looks like the figure of a person in the middle distance, difficult to see clearly in the darkness. You know that you have to walk close to this figure to get home.

As you get closer, you get the clear impression that the person you first saw vaguely from the distance is watching you, and perhaps waiting for you to get nearer. You start to feel afraid and already you feel very present in that environment—much more so than when you first saw "the watcher". You are acutely aware that you have no other way home, except to pass the figure or turn and retrace your steps—which would take a long time (and mean turning your back on the potential danger). You draw closer, ever more convinced that the figure is watching you, and that he or she has a sinister intent.

Still, you press on, heart beating fast and acutely aware of your presence in this place, with this person. Suddenly, as you get quite close to the figure, you realise that it is not, in fact, a person at all! It is a misshapen, sawn-off tree trunk and empty crate, with an old paper sack that has somehow come to be attached to the top. You relax, you walk on breathing more deeply and calmly, laughing at your own mistake, which you replay in your mind. You will tell your friends about this funny episode when you get home. You no longer feel afraid, or very present in the place.

This story of the sinister watcher, who wasn't actually there, illustrates how we can readily misperceive our environment, seeing it in different ways at different times, and that this can have profound effect on our sense of presence, of being there. In this example, high presence results from a misperception that can be understood as an illusion. But that is not to say that presence is always an illusion, it could equally be the case that the presence-inducing perception turned out to be the true one.

Perception (and presence) is partly a matter of hypothesis generation and testing. When we are fearful we tend to see what our fear predicts—as in the case of policemen mistaking a mobile phone, held by a black suspect on a dark street, for a gun. The constructivist theory of Gregory (1970) emphasised the importance of top-down processing to perception. While his view seems exaggerated in light of the clear importance of sensory information to much of perception, when that information is ambiguous our cognition appears to generate hypotheses about what might be out there to guide the perceptual process. According to our three-layer model of presence in the physical world (see Sect. 4.2, above), this corresponds to the functioning of extended presence. Top-down processing is sometimes important—but it also results in misperceptions. Gregory (1970) used it convincingly to explain how several perceptual illusions work, including the ambiguous Necker cube (Necker, 1832) shown in Fig. 3.1.

Perception, Imagination and Attention

Presence depends on perception, and here we see the importance of imagination, of top-down processing. In imagination we use metaphorical projection to make sense of what we are perceiving. But metaphor does not imply the use of imagination. Rather, imagination implies the use of metaphor, so that perception—and presence—often involves the use of metaphor. This leads us to the conclusion that our experience of any world—physical or digital—is metaphorical, in the sense that we project embodied image schemata (Johnson, 1987; Lakoff, 1987; Lakoff & Johnson, 1988) onto what we pick up as sensations to make sense of them as perceptions. When these sensations are generated or stimulated via an electronic medium, they can trigger the experience of being in another place, of a digital visit somewhere.

The top-down approach to perception of Gregory (1970) is often contrasted with the more bottom-up approach of Gibson (1966, 1972). According to Gibson, perception is largely "built-in". How we perceive things is driven, bottom-up, by innate structures. Gibson sees how we perceive as having developed over the course of evolution, and this is how we see our capacity for varying levels of presence experience. We resolve this apparent contradiction by viewing the innate structures of perception (Gibson, 1972) as another way of viewing the image schemata of Lakoff and Johnson (Johnson, 1987; Lakoff, 1987; Lakoff & Johnson, 1988). Both reflect universal human structures of meaning in experience, in imagination and through perception, reflecting the sense-data view and representationalism discussed in Chapter 2.

Presence as the Feeling of Attending to a Surrounding External World

How do we distinguish perceptions of the external world (perceptions which may themselves be largely hypothetical mental predictions) from the purely mental constructions that constitute imagined situations and events? In other words, how do we separate the internally realised world from the externally realised world? We see presence as the capacity to make this distinction and which helps us survive in a dangerous world. This is the purpose of presence (see Waterworth et al., 2015, for more details).

Waterworth et al. (2015: 36 and 48; 2020: 74) define presence as "the feeling of being located in a perceptible external world around the self", and "Varying feelings of presence reflect the extent to which attention is focused on the external environment". Presence is an experience of being in a place, one that allows us to separate the self from the non-self, the internal from the external, a faculty that helps us to survive. From this perspective, an external world—whether mediated or not—will give rise to a sense of presence, of being present in that world, in direct proportion to the extent to which the individual pays attention to that world. As Slater (2003) pointed out, presence should be distinguished from emotional engagement, but emotional engagement has an impact on presence, through its effect on level of arousal and attentional selection.

Attention to the external is important to presence in the physical world, and it is similarly important for presence in mediated worlds. We also need to believe in what is happening in a world, whether physical or not. In a mediated world, we need to provide a convincing pretence of reality for presence. But we need to attend to that pretence, and we need a reason to believe that drives our attention. We are not pretending, except in the sense that, at some level, we know the virtual reality is a simulation. But in the moment, it is real. In the moment we see the sinister watcher, we believe he is real. A moment later, we don't. This is equally true in a VR as in the physical world. Presence can be viewed as sometimes resulting from a perceptual illusion. We need to attend for an illusion to work, but only to the things that make it work. Perception can itself sometimes be illusory, in so much as we perceive something that is not as we perceive it to be.

When we feel present, we believe that what is happening is real, whether in the physical world or a VR. We do not pretend to believe, and we do not make-believe as Turner suggests. Pretence is what we do when we pay attention to fictional things, and real things too—that we know (believe) are not what we are currently perceiving in the world around our body. The form of the physical world is given, but ambiguous. In VR, we can experience fictional worlds as if they are real—in fact, as real in the moment. We believe in them and do not need to pretend that we do. Believing in the real, in-the-moment existence of something, experienced as being before us, is a characteristic of perception (and hallucinations; Smith, 2002, 2010) and of presence.

Social Interaction and Affordances for Presence

Interacting with Other People

Our discussion so far has focused mainly on the individual's experience of spatial presence, the feeling of *being there* in an environment, for instance, a physical place, other than the one in which the body is physically located. Wirth et al. (2007: 497) out this as follows: "*Spatial Presence is …the sensation of being physically situated within the spatial environment portrayed by the medium ("self-location")*". According to Sanchez-Vives and Slater (2005) the concept of spatial presence has had an impact on our understanding of human cognition and consciousness. Spatial presence involves perceptions of perceptually real environments, while social presence involves perceptions of social interactions with persons, places or things (Reno, 2005). Both are important in digital travel. Social presence, as the sense of being together with another, involves factors such as primitive responses to social cues, simulations of other minds, and automatically generated models of the intentionality of the other (Biocca et al., 2003, p. 459).

Social presence is the degree of salience or awareness of other persons in an interaction in, for instance, a virtual environment. It is the process by which people feel that they are in the presence of other people. Heeter (1992) defined it as the sense of "*being with others*". We can use tourists as an example. Tourists do not only have a spatial experience of place with buildings, nature and attractions, they often also meet other visitors and residents of a place. Tourists specifically interact in host–guest relations; that is, with employees of hospitality and tourism facilities, and also with people that they meet living or visiting there.

Horton and Wohl (1956) coined the term para-social interaction as a label for TV viewers' responses to people on the screen. According to Horton and Wohl (1956: 32): "*One of the striking characteristics of the new mass media – radio, television, and the movies – is that they give the illusion of face-to-face relationship with the performer. The conditions of response to the performer are analogous to those in a primary group*". Para-social interaction is related to social presence. Kumar and Benbasat (2002) defined para-social presence as the extent to which a medium facilitates a sense of understanding, connection, involvement and interaction among participating social entities. Giles (2002) argues that there is a correlation between para-social interaction and face-to-face interaction, but para-social interaction inevitably takes place across a distance and is entirely constrained by social and communicative conventions.

Mirrors are not only used for seeing oneself but for seeing others. To Umberto Eco (2000) TV, and in particular live broadcast, has similarities with the mirror experience. Real-time TV and mirrors are prostheses of human perception because they show things in a state of presence (Eco, 2000; Soffner, 2006).

Short, Williams and Christie (1976) developed the ideas of what they called Social Presence Theory (SPT) in the context of telecommunications. SPT is the degree to which a person is perceived to be a "real person" in their computer-mediated communication or virtual environments. Or, put another way, it describes the ability of communication media to transmit social cues. The level of social presence influences the quality of virtual interactions and outcomes. London & Hall (2011), Roberts and Sambrook (2014), Li and Wang (2013), Wu and Zhang (2014), Evans (2014, 2019) and Anderson et al. (2020) suggested that social networks and Web 2.0 tools could increase social presence in virtual business communications. The extent to which communication in a virtual environment can convey social presence will profoundly affect the quality of the digital travel experience, and the felt proximity wit people and places visited digitally.

Activities in Place: The Role of Affordances

In chapter 2 we reviewed enactivism, the view that holds that sensorimotor skills are constitutive for perception and that experiences are inseparable from the perceiver's bodily activities. In this section the focus is on the role of activity in telepresence.

Flach and Holden (1998) were among the first scholars to investigate affordance in the context of presence, by emphasising the necessity to understand the effect of interaction with objects in virtual environments. With reference to Gibson's theory, they write about virtual reality (1998: 94): *"From this perspective it is the dynamic interplay between visual, acoustic, and tactile feedback and the actions of looking around and manipulating objects that determines the fidelity of a simulation…(and)… in virtual environments the constraints on action take precedence over the constraints on perception"*.

Why do participants tend to respond realistically to situations and events portrayed within an immersive VR system? Slater (2009a) asks this question and distinguishes between immersive and non-immersive systems, arguing that in an ideal immersive system it is possible to fully simulate normal actions in physical reality. He does not use or refer to the term affordance in this paper, but what he calls correlation presence, which is the correlation(s) between activities and sensory feedback. According to Slater et al. (2009b): *"it seems that humans have a propensity to find correlations between their activity and internal state and their sense perceptions of what is going on 'out there'"*.

Presence does not demand high fidelity to physical reality, but rather that people do respond, and are able to respond, as if the sensory data transmitted by a medium were physically real. When aspects of our sensory data are being generated by a virtual reality, the perceptual system operates in exactly the same way as in an unmediated situation. The two terms, correlational presence and affordance, are closely related; the affordances offered by a virtual environment trigger and should support correlation presence (Sanchez-Vives & Slater, 2005).

Gibson, a perceptual psychologist, introduced the term affordance in his book, *The Ecological Approach to Visual Perception* (1979). His motivation was to complete the ecological theory of direct perception (Dotov et al., 2012). Since then the affordance concept has been used in a number of disciplines other than psychology, notably human–computer interaction (Hartson, 2003; Norman, 1999). Gibson claimed that we perceive objects as having properties of what we ought to do with them and attributes full normativity to affordances. Affordances are not properties of what we should do with an object, but what we can do with it. User interfaces can offer perceptible affordances (Gaver, 1991), since they can offer information about virtual objects that can be acted upon. A perceptible affordance is a perceptual cue to the function of an object that causes an action. For instance, a visual presentation contains visual information about the behavioural possibilities afforded to the user. It is this action and behavioural aspect that the affordance concept captures.

In tourism, sightseeing is a common activity. A perceptible affordance queries what activity a particular sightseer would like to engage in at a particular moment in time. There are a number of actions that can provide perceptible affordance in sightseeing when it takes place in a VE. Consider viewing an attraction on the screen, for instance, a tourist who gazes at an historic monument and at that moment thinks, "I will walk to the front door and enter the building through that door". According to Morie et al. (2005) all affordances are user contingent; in a VE they are essentially triggers that might result in an action (physical response) or a reaction (emotional response) from the participant. Sensory data play a key role.

A video game context can simultaneously enable the perception of action, when watching images on a screen while sitting passively in a chair. Another example might be a website for a destination developed for marketing purposes. In this marketing context we can ask: what is the effect of this website on the user? An interview may reveal that one user of the website considers the portrayed destination to be beautiful, while another person who looks at the same website decides it is time to book accommodation, find out how to get there, and search for events and what to do upon arrival. It is this second example that corresponds to the notion of perceptible affordance. In both cases, the notion of transparency discussed above, of not noticing the technology producing the experience, is a key part of the affordance-action loop.

But how do we operationalise affordance? Few empirical studies have operationalised affordance in a VR context. One example from an e-commerce study is Algharabat and Dennis (2010) who operationalise virtual affordance as follows: "*3D let me feel like as if I am holding a real laptop and rotating it*". In Chapter 5 we present two experimental studies which, among other factors, looked closely at the importance of affordances in a digital tourism context. Additionally, we present new findings on the view people have of the possibilities and desirability of digital travel, gathered by survey during the COVID-19 pandemic with the attendant hazards and restrictions on physical travel.

Implications For Digital Travel

Telepresence is the experience of being somewhere other than one's physical location, and can be achieved through digital media, perhaps *only* through digital media. It is tantamount to experiencing a sense of place through digital technology. The main focus of the chapter was thus to compare and contrast different current theoretical accounts of telepresence, in the light of their plausibility and implications for understanding in what ways people can experience a sense of being in a place other than their physical location, and with other people. These accounts included presence as a pretence (a simulation of reality), as pretending (making believe the virtual world is real), as a perceptual illusion ("the illusion of non-mediation") and as embodied attention to the surrounding (or apparently surrounding) environment. These views are all well-accepted in the field, and all can be seen as contributing to a virtual travel experience, which is itself a kind of illusion.

Our argument was informed by the Spinozian model of rapid acceptance response introduced in Chapter 2—we initially believe (accept as real) any argument (experience) that we can understand, then may reassess and reach a more settled judgment once the moment has passed. In line with this, as we saw in Chapter 2, presence itself is seen as a Type-1, an intuitive, perceptual process. But digital travel is more than just feeling present in a mediated environment, in the moment.

Travel is usually planned and is always reflected upon after the event. During a trip, and while making a visit, our expectations and earlier reflections will influence the nature of the experience, as will our meetings with people and the activities we engage in. Afterwards, we will reflect further, telling ourselves and others about our experiences. What we remember will be to some extent a function of how present we feel in a place, whether the place is physical or digitally created—this is a key aspect of the power of presence and its significance for digital travel.

When we feel highly present, we believe in the perceived world in which we experience ourselves to be. In that moment it is real to us. Creating that effect is a key part of a convincing digital travel experience. To have that experience, we must be attending to the digital world, feeling as if we are (as-if-physically) surrounded by it. When that is achieved, our imaginations are involved in at least two ways: in how we perceive our surroundings, and in how we conceptualise our being there. While we do not think that we need to make-believe (that the world is real), we do use our imagination, and memory, to make sense of what happens there. The world may be a simulation, be veridical, be misperceived or even be an hallucination. In the moment we do not reflect on this question, and so we do not know which it is—but we believe that it *is*. And when we later reflect and talk about our experience, it is as if it were real—which, to us, it was.

References

Algharabat, R., & Dennis, C. (2010). Using authentic 3D product visualisation for an electrical online retailer. *Journal of Customer Behaviour, 9*(2), 97–115. https://doi.org/10.1362/147539210X511326

Anderson, V., Gifford, J., & Wildman, J. (2020). An evaluation of social learning and learner outcomes in a massive open online course (MOOC): A healthcare sector case study. *Human Resource Development International, 23*(3), 208–237.

Artaud, A. (1938). *The theatre and its double*. Grove Press.

Biocca, F., Harms, C., & Burgoon, J. K. (2003). Toward a More robust theory and measure of social presence: Review and suggested criteria. *Presence: Teleoperators and Virtual Environments, 12*(5), 456–480. https://doi.org/10.1162/105474603322761270

Byrne, A. (2009). Experience and content. *The Philosophical Quarterly, 59*(236), 429–451. https://doi.org/10.1111/j.1467-9213.2009.614.x

Codognet, P. (2003). *Artificial natura and natural artifice*. MIT Press.

Cummings, J. J., & Bailenson, J. N. (2016). How immersive is enough? A meta-analysis of the effect of immersive technology on user presence. *Media Psychology, 19*(2), 272–309. https://doi.org/10.1080/15213269.2015.1015740

Da Pos, O. (1997). *Visual perception and colour illusion* (pp. 34–41). The Color Science Association of Japan.

Da Pos, O. (2008). A phenomenological instead of a psychophysical definition of visual illusions. *Gestalt Theory, 30*(2), 181–190.

Da Pos, O., & Zambianchi, E. (1996). Visual illusions and effects: A collection. In *Visual illusions and effects: A collection.*

Deleuze, G. (1994). *Difference and repetition*. Columbia University Press.

Dotov, D. G., Nie, L., & de Wit, M. M. (2012). Understanding affordances: History and contemporary development of Gibson's central concept. *Avant: Trends in Interdisciplinary Studies, 3*(2), 28–39.

Eco, U. (2000). *Kant and the platypus: Essays on language and cognition*. Harcourt Brace.

Etzioni, A., & Etzioni, O. (1999). Face-to-face and computer-Mediated communities, a comparative analysis. *The Information Society, 15*(4), 241–248. https://doi.org/10.1080/019722499128402

Evans, P. (2014). Exploring the relationship between discourse and a practice perspective on HRD in a virtual environment. *Human Resource Development International, 17*(2), 183–202. https://doi.org/10.1080/13678868.2014.886889

Evans, P. (2019). Making an HRD domain: Identity work in an online professional community. *Human Resource Development International, 22*(2), 116–139. https://doi.org/10.1080/13678868.2018.1564514

Flach, J., & Holden, J. (1998). The reality of experience: Gibson's way. *Presence: Teleoperators and virtual environments*. https://doi.org/10.1162/105474698565550

Gaver, W. W. (1991). Technology affordances. *Proceedings of the SIGCHI Conference on Human Factors in Computing Systems Reaching through Technology—CHI '91*, 79–84. https://doi.org/10.1145/108844.108856

Gibson, J. J. (1966). *The senses considered as perceptual systems*. Houghton Mifflin.

Gibson, J. J. (1972). A theory of direct visual perception. In J. Royce, W. Rozenboom (Eds.), *The psychology of knowing*. Gordon & Breach.

Gibson, J. J. (1979). *The ecological approach to visual perception: Classic edition* (1st ed.). Psychology Press. https://doi.org/10.4324/9781315740218

Giles, D. C. (2002). Parasocial interaction: A review of the literature and a model for future research. *Media Psychology, 4*(3), 279–305. https://doi.org/10.1207/S1532785XMEP0403_04

Gregory, R. L. (1970). *The intelligent eye*. McGraw-Hill.

Hartson, R. (2003). Cognitive, physical, sensory, and functional affordances in interaction design. *Behaviour & Information Technology, 22*(5), 315–338. https://doi.org/10.1080/01449290310001592587

Heeter, C. (1992). 'Being-i-There': The subjective experience of presence. *Presence: Teleoperators and Virtual Environments, 1*(2), 262–271. https://doi.org/10.1162/pres.1992.1.2.262

Horton, D., & Richard Wohl, R. (1956). Mass communication and para-social interaction: Observations on intimacy at a distance. *Psychiatry, 19*(3), 215–229. https://doi.org/10.1080/00332747.1956.11023049

Ihde, D. (2002). *Bodies in technologies*. University of Minnesota Press.

Johnson, M. (1987). *The body in the mind: The bodily basis of meaning, imagination, and reason*. University of Chicago Press.

Kumar, N., & Benbasat, I. (2002). Para-social presence and communication capabilities of a web site: A theoretical perspective. *E-Service Journal, 1*(2), 5–24.

Lakoff, G. (1987). *Woman, fire and dangerous things: What categories reveal about the mind*. University of Chicago Press.
Lakoff, G., & Johnson, M. (1988). *Metaphors we live by*. University of Chicago Press.
Lee, K. M. (2004). Presence, explicated. *Communication Theory, 14*(1), 27–50. https://doi.org/10.1111/j.1468-2885.2004.tb00302.x
Li, Y., & Wang, Y. (2013). Social Influence from personalized recommendations to trusting beliefs of websites: Intermediate role of social presence. In P. Kotzé, G. Marsden, G. Lindgaard, J. Wesson, & M. Winckler (Eds.), *Human-computer interaction—INTERACT 2013* (Vol. 8119, pp. 632–639). Springer Berlin Heidelberg. https://doi.org/10.1007/978-3-642-40477-1_42
Lombard, M., & Ditton, T. (1997). At the heart of it all: The concept of presence. *Journal of Computer-Mediated Communication, 3*(2). https://doi.org/10.1111/j.1083-6101.1997.tb00072.x
London, M., & Hall, M. J. (2011). Web 2.0 support for individual, group and organizational learning. *Human Resource Development International, 14*(1), 103–113. https://doi.org/10.1080/13678868.2011.542902
Merleau-Ponty, M. (1962). *Phenomenology of perception* (1962 [Paris: Gallimard, 1945]). Routledge and Kegan Paul.
Minsky, M. (1980). Telepresence. *Omni Magazine*, 44–52.
Morie, J. F., Williams, J., Dozois, A., & Luigi, D.-P. (2005). The fidelity of 'feel': Emotional affordance in virtual environments. In *Proceedings of the 11th International Conference on Human-Computer Interaction*.
Necker, L. A. (1832). Observations on some remarkable optical phenomena seen in Switzerland; and on an optical phenomenon which occurs on viewing a figure of a crystal or geometrical solid. *The London and Edinburgh Philosophical Magazine and Journal of Science, 1*(5), 329–337.
Norman, D. A. (1999). Affordance, conventions, and design. *Interactions, 6*(3), 38–43. https://doi.org/10.1145/301153.301168
Polanyi, M. (1966). *The tacit dimension*. The University of Chicago Press.
Reno´, L. A. (2005). Presence and mediated spaces: A review. *PsychNology Journal, 3*, 181–199.
Reynolds, R. I. (1988). A psychological definition of illusion. *Philosophical Psychology, 1*(2), 217–223. https://doi.org/10.1080/09515088808572940
Riva, G. (1999). From technology to communication: Psycho-social issues in developing virtual environments. *Journal of Visual Languages & Computing, 10*(1), 87–97. https://doi.org/10.1006/jvlc.1998.0110
Roberts, G., & Sambrook, S. (2014). Social networking and HRD. *Human Resource Development International, 17*(5), 577–587. https://doi.org/10.1080/13678868.2014.969504

Sanchez-Vives, M. V., & Slater, M. (2005). From presence to consciousness through virtual reality. *Nature Reviews Neuroscience, 6*(4), 332–339. https://doi.org/10.1038/nrn1651

Sas, C., & O'Hare, G. M. P. (2003). Presence equation: An investigation into cognitive factors underlying presence. *Presence: Teleoperators and Virtual Environments, 12*(5), 523–537. https://doi.org/10.1162/105474603322761315

Schloerb, D. W. (1995). A quantitative measure of telepresence. *Presence: Teleoperators and Virtual Environments, 4*(1), 64–80. https://doi.org/10.1162/pres.1995.4.1.64

Schudson, M. (1978). The ideal of conversation in the study of mass media. *Communication Research, 5*(3), 320–329. https://doi.org/10.1177/009365027800500306

Short, J., Williams, E., & Bruce, C. (1976). *The social psychology of telecommunications*. Wiley.

Slater, M. (2002). Understanding virtual environments: Immersion, presence, and performance. In *ACM Siggraph 2002*, San Antonio, TX.

Slater, M. (2003). A note on presence terminology. *Presence Connect, 3*(3), 1–5.

Slater, M. (2009). Place illusion and plausibility can lead to realistic behaviour in immersive virtual environments. *Philosophical Transactions of the Royal Society b: Biological Sciences, 364*(1535), 3549–3557. https://doi.org/10.1098/rstb.2009.0138

Slater, M., Lotto, B., Arnold, M. M., & Sacnhez-Vives, M. V. (2009). How we experience immersive virtual environments: The concept of presence and its measurement. *Anuario De Psicología, 40*(2), 193–210.

Smith, A. D. (2002). *The problem of perception*. Harvard University Press.

Smith, A. D. (2010). Disjunctivism and illusion. *Philosophy and Phenomenological Research, 80*(2), 384–410.

Söffner, J. (2006). What production of presence and mimesis have in common. In *Proceedings of the 9th international workshop on presence*.

Turner, P., Turner, S., & Carruthers, L. (2014). It's not interaction, it's make believe. *Proceedings of the 2014 European Conference on Cognitive Ergonomics—ECCE '14*, 1–8. https://doi.org/10.1145/2637248.2637266

Turner, S., Huang, C.-W., Burrows, L., & Turner, P. (2016). Make-believing virtual realities. In P. Turner & J. T. Harviainen (Eds.), *Digital make-believe* (pp. 27–47). Springer International Publishing. https://doi.org/10.1007/978-3-319-29553-4_3

Voss, C. (2011). Film experience and the formulation of illusion: The spectator as 'surrogate body' for the cinema. *Cinema Journal, 50*(4), 136–150.

Waterworth, J. A., Chignell, M., & Moller, H. (2020). Age-sensitive well-being support. In *Technology and health* (pp. 67–88). Elsevier. https://doi.org/10.1016/B978-0-12-816958-2.00004-6

Waterworth, J. A., & Riva, G. (2014). *Feeling present in the physical world and in computer-mediated environments*. Palgrave Macmillan.

Waterworth, J. A., Waterworth, E. L., Riva, G., & Mantovani, F. (2015). Presence: Form, content and consciousness. In M. Lombard, F. Biocca, J. Freeman, W. IJsselsteijn, & R. J. Schaevitz (Eds.), *Immersed in media* (pp. 35–58). Springer International Publishing. https://doi.org/10.1007/978-3-319-10190-3_3

Wirth, W., Hartmann, T., Böcking, S., Vorderer, P., Klimmt, C., Schramm, H., Saari, T., Laarni, J., Ravaja, N., Gouveia, F. R., Biocca, F., Sacau, A., Jäncke, L., Baumgartner, T., & Jäncke, P. (2007). A process model of the formation of spatial presence experiences. *Media Psychology, 9*(3), 493–525. https://doi.org/10.1080/15213260701283079

Wu, F., & Zhang, X. (2014). Employees' positions in virtual working community and their job performances: A social network analysis. *Human Resource Development International, 17*(2), 231–242. https://doi.org/10.1080/13678868.2014.891309

Open Access This chapter is licensed under the terms of the Creative Commons Attribution 4.0 International License (http://creativecommons.org/licenses/by/4.0/), which permits use, sharing, adaptation, distribution and reproduction in any medium or format, as long as you give appropriate credit to the original author(s) and the source, provide a link to the Creative Commons license and indicate if changes were made.

The images or other third party material in this chapter are included in the chapter's Creative Commons license, unless indicated otherwise in a credit line to the material. If material is not included in the chapter's Creative Commons license and your intended use is not permitted by statutory regulation or exceeds the permitted use, you will need to obtain permission directly from the copyright holder.

CHAPTER 4

Visiting Places

Abstract In this chapter we look at notions of place, as outlined in work in human geography, tourism studies and other applied social fields. We consider the distinction between spaces and places and on how different experiences of place arise in the traveller. This is important to our understanding of tourist and other travel experiences, and to experiencing a sense of place in digital environments. Despite some commonalities, we find that digital travel is unlike physical travel in many significant respects, but that the experience of a place can, in some circumstances, be similar. For digital travel and digital experiences, place attachment is relevant for places that a person knows well. We conclude that a digital experience can become a spatial experience if our bodily senses are invoked by the virtual place.

Keywords Place · Tourism · Human geography · Insideness · Hedonic consumption

INTRODUCTION

Digital technology can be used to create a fantasy world (Book, 2003), and also to replicate a place that actually exists. If a digital environment replicates a place a person could physically visit, what experience is created and how can we understand it? This is an underlying theme of the book. In the last chapter, we examined various views and findings on the sense of being present in another place, other than the place where the physical body is located. We presented this as a key distinction between physical travel and digital travel: the location of the traveller's physical body.

In this chapter we examine different notions of place, as outlined in work in tourism studies and other applied social fields; how and when different experiences of place arise for the traveller. We also stress that virtual travel is unlike physical travel in many significant respects, drawing on well-established theoretical accounts of travel emphasising the importance for the overall travel experience of experiencing departure from the present place (home), the journey itself and the process of arrival (and "incorporation") at a distal place.

Several authors have suggested that the ever-expanding move of society towards electronic communication in some ways destroys the sense of place underlying many social interactions, social conventions and rituals. In critically discussing this view, we are influenced by the social geographer Relph, who reinterpreted the person–environment relationship and how individuals experience a place phenomenologically. We discuss the value of how Relph (1976) defines experience of places as *"fusions of human and natural order ... [places are] the significant centers of our immediate experiences of the world"*.

A place can be somewhere we leave, and also somewhere we arrive. Between is the journey, the travel (from the French *travail*), the work that takes us from the former to the later. At the place of arrival, the traveller needs to be assimilated into the place, and this is only fully possible when the necessary cues are "in place". Insights into the assimilation process are drawn from the second-home literature, among other sources.

As a step to integrating the contributions from different authors, we present a framework later in the chapter for evaluating the extent to which we can describe a digital travel experience as an actual travel experience. We distinguish between the pre-trip phase, the travel and *being there* phase and the post-visit phase. The key question is: to what extent and in what ways is the digital experience similar to or different from the in situ experience? In some cases, they are, or are perceived, as different. In other cases, the answer is that there is weak relationship to the actual in situ experience, or a strong one—it is a similar experience.

Sense of Place

Spaces and Places

The term destination is frequently used in the travel literature. Most often it refers to a geographical place. Space is related term, as in public or private spaces. What is the difference between a space and a place? According to Mingers (2001), we experience space in terms of objects and their relations to each other—*next to, on top of, beside*—and so on. To Harrison and Dourish (1996) the relationship between place and space is essentially a distinction between two accounts of spaces. The first is an experiential while the second is geometrical (Brewer & Dourish, 2008). Ciolfi (2004) uses the terms in a similar manner. He defines place as experienced space, and place is also often used as a geographical term, indicating what occupies a location.

The social aspect is one of the key components in all human experiences, and for sense of place. Meyrowitz (1986) observed that modern communication media commonly lack the sense of place that would frame the social behaviours of people meeting physically. People may have what seem to be face-to-face encounters, and yet they are not, since the participants are in different physical places. They do not share an experience of being in the same place and they behave in ways that would be inappropriate if they did—their behaviour is "out of place". Lentini and Decortis (2010: 408) write *"Sense of place refers to how people apprehend physical space not only through the perception of its spatial characteristics, but also through the awareness of the social cues related to it"*. The history of a place, what is it known for, events that have happened there or are going to happen there, is also part of the place construct.

Human Geography and Edwards Relph's Place Theory

In his inaugural editorial of *Tourism Geographies*, Alan Lew (1999) pointed out that the field of tourism research is characterised by an over-representation of studies that bear a geographic orientation. This is not surprising since the concept of place is one of the core constructs in human geography (Kaltenborn, 1998). Tourists visit places. Therefore, it is reasonable that destinations and attractions represent core subjects in the tourism research terminology (Tribe & Xiao, 2011).

Geographers commonly use the term *sense of place*. It is a relational concept (Sack, 1992) that must be understood within the context of human—environment relationships. Kaltenborn (1998) argues that the meaning of place is not inherent in the properties of nature, but rather interpreted and constructed by humans in particular contexts and situations. For Cheng et al. (2003) place emerges in the intersection of three spheres: social and political processes, the physical, and social and cultural meanings.

In most cases, geographers study residents and not visitors, but sense of place is also relevant in the context of tourism. In tourism, there is stream of research on visits to outdoor environments such as national parks (Kyle & Chick, 2007; Williams et al., 1992; Williams & Vaske, 2003). One of the central concepts used by Williams, Kyle and others is place attachment; that is, a bond that a person might have to a particular place. Researchers in human geography use the concept of place attachment to explain why people visit the same recreational park again and again. Also, researchers on the topic of second homes (e.g. Jaakson, 1986) use place attachment to understand the place experience (Gustafson, 2001; Stedman, 2006; Williams & Kaltenborn, 1999). For digital travel and digital experiences, place attachment can be a relevant concept for places that a person knows well.

The term *tourism experience* is frequently used, but is not a term commonly used by geographers who, according to Li (2000), prefer the term *"geographical consciousness"* to relate to the human experience of space, place and the aesthetic elements of a place. Li (2000) argues that the concept of geographical consciousness has been overlooked by tourism research although it is closely related to the tourism experience. Li adds that insights from geographers, particularly Edward Relph and Yi-Fu Tuan, are relevant for the field of tourism because *"tourism experience is intimately joined with a tourist's cognition such as geographical consciousness"* (Li, 2000: 877).

Relph is the author of the frequently cited monograph *Place and Placelessness* (1976). According to Seamon (1982), Relph reinterprets phenomenologically the person–environment relationship and how individuals experience a place. Relph defines experience of places as *"fusions of human and natural order ... [places are] the significant centers of our immediate experiences of the world"* (p. 141). His insideness–outsideness concept reflects the nature of one's involvement with a place. It is reasonable to argue that for a place experience the insideness types of experience are more relevant and fit better for residents than visitors while the outsideness types are more relevant for and have a better fit with visitors than residents. Relph's seven types of place experience are presented in Table 4.1.

Building on Relph's work, the sociologist Gustafson (2001) proposed a three-pole triangular model with the components self, environment and others. Turner and Turner (2006) applied Gustafson's model in a VR context. They argued that when studying virtual applications, and in particular those that mirror the physical world, Gustafson's model and Relph's theory both seem appropriate. Gustafson, however, emphasises people, the life of the people living in a place, and to a lesser extent the physical environment. A place is a phenomenon by which their behaviour can be described, explained and predicted (Snepenger et al., 2007).

The philosopher Edward Casey (2001) distinguished between dwelling as residing and dwelling as wandering, and also emphasised bodily engagement. Casey defines place in consonance with Merleau-Ponty's term "lived body". To Merleau-Ponty the lived body consists in an *I can*, a practical engagement in the world. According to Casey (2001: 718)

Table 4.1 Relph's seven types of place experience

Edward Relph's Place Theory

Existential insideness: Feeling of attachment and being at home, experience of place as full of meanings without self-conscious reflection	**Existential outsideness**: Sense of not belonging, feeling of separation, alienation, lack of meanings and (reflective) un-involvement
Behavioral insideness: The place is perceived as objects and activities. Awareness of the distinctiveness of the place and engagement with the place	**Objective outsideness**: Place is a thing to be studied and manipulated A dispassionate attitude, a separation and distance between person and place
Empathetic insideness: A concern for and interest in the place, but not necessarily directly involved with or agreeing to the meaning of the place (to others)	**Incidental outsideness**: Place is experienced as incidental background for activities, what the person is doing overshadows where the person is
Vicarious insideness: Experience of place in a secondhand or vicarious way without physically visiting the place, the person is involved with the place, a transportation through imagination	

"*only the body holds together, in one coherent entity, the sense of place, the past pertinent to that place (that is, via body memories), and the orienting power which place requires. The body is the only aspect of our being - individual or collective - capable of performing place, that is to say, making place a living reality*". Seamon (2018: 14) comments that Merleau-Ponty says little about the significance of place directly, but: "*his perspective does much to clarify its integral relationship with the lived body and human situatedness*".

For digital travel and digital experiences, a focus on the body might at first been seen as irrelevant. We suggested in Chapter 3 that what distinguishes digital travel is that the traveller's body can be seen as being left behind. But this is only half the story. In our discussion of Merleau-Ponty, and research that build his theoretical contributions, we saw the importance of evoking bodily reactions. A digital experience can be a spatial experience and our bodily senses are then invoked by the virtual place. In digital travel, the body is located in one physical place, but at least some embodied sensory experiences are invoked somewhere else—in a digital place.

Marketing and Hedonic Consumption

Tourists are, or most often can be seen as, consumers. Consumers may process information from either a hedonic or a utilitarian perspective depending on their goals (Pham, 1998; Shiv & Fedorikhin, 1999). In the marketing literature, the two articles by Holbrook and Hirschman (1982) and Hirschman and Holbrook (1982) on hedonic consumption are seminal. According to Hirschman and Holbrook (1986: 219), consumption experience is "*an emergent property that results from a complex system of mutually overlapping interrelationships in constant reciprocal interaction with personal, environmental, and situational inputs*". It is the synthesis of the affective and cognitive actions and reactions that consumers have during their interface with products, services and the environment of the marketplace.

The articles by Holbrook and Hirschman have had an influence on the field of tourism marketing because the tourism experience emphasises experiential aspects of visiting places. For some travellers, hedonic might describe quite well what they do and seek on their vacation. For others, utilitarian aspects might be more important. Some visitors also develop an affective connection with specific places or destinations

(Giuliani & Feldman, 1993; Hidalgo & Hernandez, 2001). The experiential qualities of a tourist destination's offerings are something that tourism marketers recognise as significant for travellers. Shopping is a common tourist activity, and therefore hedonic and utilitarian consumption have been used to capture and analyse shopping as a tourism activity (Jones et al., 2006).

Some researchers conceive and conceptualise a tourist destination as an amalgam of components that form a holistic experience of the place visited (Murphy et al., 2000). Tourism is often referred to as a hedonic consumption experience (Govers & Go, 2005; Govers et al., 2007; Vogt & Fesenmaier, 1998). Snepenger et al. (2004) investigated the meanings associated with a spectrum of tourism places. They found that tourism places could be differentiated in terms of their normative, hedonic, utilitarian, social and consumption meanings. Snepenger et al., (2004: 115) posit that places serve distinct functions in people's lives and "*the greater the tourism demand for a place, the more hedonic the normative meanings of experiences at the place*".

Investigations of the hedonic and utilitarian components of consumption have been addressed in various disciplines including advertising. In advertising research, it is not uncommon to use virtual environments or virtual applications (Ping et al., 2010; Goh et al., 2014). Some researchers in this field use the term "*advergames*". According to Dahl et al. (2009), an advergame tries to offer consumers an interactive entertainment so that the player may form an emotional connection between the game and the brand featured within it. In a recent paper by Speilmann et al. (2018), respondents (in several studies) were instructed to think about the last memorable experience they had when traveling to a destination. Based on the empirical results and analysis, the authors proposed a place authenticity scale. A key element in a memorable experience concept is realness, which concerns the availability of believable facts and accuracy in rendition. These factors play a similar role in a digital experience as in an in situ experience.

There are many interesting findings from advergame studies, and one conclusion is that it makes sense to use games and 3D environments for product placement, advertising research and shopper studies (Jiang & Benbasat, 2004; Lau et al., 2014). While some of the researchers give explicit tasks to the participants in the advergame, for instance, to do shopping, others do not give any tasks besides using the game application. When designing a study for virtual environments as tourist locations, it is relevant to build on these advergames studies because they typically focus on behavioural intention and experiential aspects.

Intention to Visit a Place and Word of Mouth
In an e-commerce context, purchase intentions have been used in several studies (Ahn & Bailenson, 2011; Chen et al., 2019; Griffith & Chen, 2004; Jiang & Benbasat, 2007; Kim & Shim, 2002; Li et al., 2002, 2003; Suh & Chang, 2006) to gauge later behaviour. The equivalent in a tourism context is the intention to visit a place or destination. The vividness of information can sometimes but not always increase its persuasive power (Taylor & Thompson, 1982) and a direct experience can influence persuasion (Fazio & Zanna, 1978; Wu & Shaffer, 1987), and therefore intention to purchase and, presumably, intention to visit a place.

In consumer research, word of mouth (WoM) is a well-established concept (Arndt, 1967; Richins, 1983) to help predict purchase intentions. Word of mouth is defined by Anderson (1998) and Singh (1988) as all informal communications between a customer and others regarding evaluations of goods or services. The WoM concept is also used in studies of service industries (Maxham, 2001; Yu & Dean, 2001) and a number of other fields (Schmäh et al., 2017). In tourism there seems to be a preference for the terms recommendation- and destination-WoM (Bigne et al., 2001; Simpson & Siguaw, 2008). Both concepts, intention to visit and word of mouth, are viewed as relevant and useful for empirical studies of the phenomena in question.

Experiencing Sense of Place in a Virtual Environment

Smyth et al. (2015) conceptualised the virtual experience of place in a way that contains the same components as or proposed in Relph's model of place. However, in Smyth et al.'s model, physical aspects, affective experiences and activities are all mediated by technology. It is not possible to reproduce the exact experience of being in a physical place, but Smyth et al. argue that it is possible to produce a convincing illusion of non-mediation, a feeling of being there. In Chapter 3 we discussed several different current interpretations of the factors involved in the creation of this kind of illusion.

Traditionally, human geography has not focused on the role of technology, the experience of a place with or through media, but in telepresence research there is some interest in human geography. Turner et al. (2005: 10) argue that "*Relph's discussion of 'insideness' and 'outsideness' offers a compelling insight for contextualizing the VR experience*". They discuss insideness and outsideness in relationship to Heidegger's concept of dwelling. To Heidegger, dwelling is our thought about our relation to space. Shamai (1991) finds Relph's distinction between seven different degrees of outsideness and insideness in ways of sensing a place practical and useful. Shamai (1991: 349) writes:

> Each different way of sensing the place can be seen as a different level on an ordinal scale; that is, starting with the lowest level of sense of place and 'climbing' up six more steps to reach the most intense and deepest way of sensing a place.

Relph uses the term vicarious insideness (Table 4.1), although very few tourism researchers use the concept of vicariousness. However, one work that does include the concept of vicariousness is of particular relevance for virtual tourism: *Vicarious Journeys: Travels in Music* (Connell & Gibson, 2004: 7). The authors observe that "*many albums from the 1950s and 1960s attempted to 'capture' the sounds of far-away places, vicariously transporting the armchair listener to idyllic holiday destinations, mysterious Pacific Islands, Alpine heights or cosmopolitan European streetscapes*". The term "*vicariously transporting*" is of interest, and not only for what music can do, but as suggesting an experience induced by media technology. Destinations can influence image formation through secondary place interactions with consumers, so-called vicarious experiences (Kim & Richardson, 2003).

McCarthy and Wright (2005: 921) in their discussion of technology, space and the experience of place write:

> But people can also have a sense of place as they wander. People can in some meaningful way dwell in public spaces like arcades and parks as they move about them, shopping or just hanging out. People can clearly have a strong sense of place about a city as they wander around its winding streets. Increasingly, people dwell on street-corners and in the buses, trains or cars in which they spend hours travelling to and from work. But the experience of wandering can be considered dwelling only if the people involved feel settled. In contrast, if people's wandering is exploratory, if they are trying

to find a place, get oriented, or simply moving between places, there is no dwelling or being in place.

Although not many in telepresence research have built on human geography, it is reasonable to reflect on and apply concepts from this field in studies of the feeling of *being there* and ask: just how is the body part of a telepresence experience? Raymond et al. (2017) refer to Evans and Stanovich's dual process theory in their discussion on affordance in sense of place research. Raymond et al. (2017: 5) write: "it remains unclear how the *immediately perceived and sensory dimensions* of sight, smell, hearing, taste, and touch (i.e. aspects of sensory experience) contribute to overall place meaning (2017: 5)". A recent study by Buzova et al. (2020) focused on sensory perceptions of how tourists evaluate their place experiences, based on a lexical analysis of blogs, and seeks to unpack the role of the senses in visitors' destination evaluations. As we saw in Chapter 3, the experience of presence is best understood as an example of Type-1 processing: as immediate, instinctive and un-reflective. When we are preoccupied with trying to work out where we are, and how to find our way somewhere else, we engage in primarily Type-2 processing—more logical and reflective. Our attention is channelled in such a way that we are not so aware of actually being there, of dwelling, in the current place.

Insights from Non-digital Travel and Tourism

In Chapters 2 and 3 we discussed aspects of feeling one is somewhere and the digital experience of *being there* in another place. But the telepresence experience cannot be understood without a reference to the travel and tourism experiences to places in situ. In this section, we look more closely at the travel and tourism perspective, of *being there* in situ. Below we draw attention to the work of the sociologist Eric Cohen (1972, 1979) and to tourism as an activity that is intrinsically motivated and can be studied from the individual traveller's point of view (Mannell & Iso-Ahola, 1987; Pearce, 1991).

Cohen (1979) identified five modes of tourism experience: recreational, diversionary, experiential mode and existential modes. The first two, the recreational mode and the diversionary mode, are particularly relevant to our discussion. The recreational mode emphasises that the individual tourist steps outside the normal, the ordinary, in search of entertainment. It is well known that many tourists take part in activities that can be characterised as entertainment, such as visiting scenic places, visiting famous restaurants, and engaging in situational leisure activities. The second is the diversionary mode. The motivation here is to break out of the daily routines and stress of everyday life for a short while, by going to another place and not having the same routines and obligations.

As a step to integrating Cohen's contributions and those of other key authors in the field, we present (Table 4.2) a framework for evaluating the extent to which we can describe a digital travel experience as an actual travel experience. We distinguish between the pre-trip phase, the travel, the *being there* phase and the post-visit phase.

Tjostheim developed and tested an extended version of Edward Relph's types of placeness that included behavioural outsideness and vicarious outsideness (Tjostheim, 2020; see Table 4.3). As with Cohen's distinction between recreational or diversionary tourism experience, the three categories of outsideness—incidental, behavioural and vicarious outsideness—can serve as a counterpart, a yardstick to make sense of the telepresence experience. In Chapter 5 we report results from the use of a measure that included these additional types, to shed more light on the role of sense of place in digital travel experiences.

Conclusions

In this chapter we have examined notions of place, as outlined in work in tourism studies and other applied social fields and on how and when different experiences of place arise in the traveller. The distinction between spaces and places, and experiencing a sense of place, are important to our understanding of tourist and other travel experiences. These insights can be generalised to experiencing a sense of place in digital environments. Marketing and the notion of hedonic consumption are also useful in understanding travel and travellers, for example, through their intention to visit a place and provide word of mouth recommendations about it.

The tourist experience is an amalgam of different experiences. It involves all senses and therefore their impact should not be overlooked in efforts to theorise tourism's experiential dimensions (Dann & Jacobsen, 2002, 2003; Edensor, 2006; Franklin & Crang, 2001; Rickly-Boyd, 2009: 269, Ryan, 2010).

A key question concerns the extent and ways in which a digital experience similar to or different from the in situ experience. Virtual travel is

Table 4.2 Framework for evaluating the extent to which a digital travel experience can be seen as an actual travel experience (bold indicates the most relevant)

In situ	Digital		
	The pre-trip phase, the anticipation of the travel experience	The travel phase, the *being there* Experience	The post-visit phase: remember and sharing the experience with others
Relph (1976)			
Existential insideness	No	No	No
Empathetic insideness	No	No	No
Behavioural insideness	No	No	No
Vicarious insideness	No or weak	No or weak	No or weak
Objective outsideness	No	No	No
Incidental outsideness	Weak or similar to	Weak or similar to	No or weak
Vicarious outsideness	Weak or similar to	Weak or similar to	Weak
Behavioral outsideness	Weak or similar to	Weak or similar to	Weak
Existential outsideness	No	No	No
Cohen (1979)			
Recreational mode	Weak or similar to	Weak or similar to	No or weak
Diversionary mode	Weak or similar to	Weak or similar to	No or weak
Experiential mode	No	No	No
Experimental mode	No	No	No
Existential mode	No	No	No
Holbrook and Hirschman (1982)			
Utilitarian components	Weak	No	No
Hedonic components	Weak or similar to	Weak or similar to	Weak

Table 4.3 Relph's types of sense of place with two new types of outsideness

Relph's Place Theory including two new types (in colour)	**Objective outsideness**: Place is a thing to be studied and manipulated. A dispassionate attitude, a separation and distance between person and place
Existential insideness: Feeling of attachment and being at home, experience of place as full of meanings without self-conscious reflection	**Incidental outsideness**: Place is experienced as incidental background for activities, what the person is doing overshadows where the person is
Empathetic insideness: A concern for and interest in the place, but not necessarily directly involved with or agreeing to the meaning of the place (to others)	**Behavioral outsideness**: The place is perceived as objects and activities. Awareness of the distinctiveness of the place, but focus on myself, my interests and activities
Behavioral insideness: The place is perceived as objects and activities. Awareness of the distinctiveness of the place and engagement with the place	**Vicarious outsideness**: Experience of place in a secondhand or vicarious way without physically visiting the place. The place is primarily a background for activities
Vicarious insideness: Experience of place in a secondhand or vicarious way without physically visiting the place the person is involved with the place, a transportation through imagination	**Existential outsideness**: Sense of not belonging, feeling of separation, alienation, lack of meanings and (reflective) un-involvement

unlike physical travel in many significant respects, but the experience of a place—once one has the feeling of *being there*—may be more or less similar. For digital travel and digital experiences, place attachment can be a relevant concept for places that a person knows well. And a digital experience can become a spatial experience if our bodily senses are invoked in the virtual place. A key element in a memorable experience is perceived realness. Facts and accuracy play a similar role in digital experiences as in in situ experiences, as we shall see in the next chapter.

References

Ahn, S. J., & Bailenson, J. N. (2011). Self-endorsing versus other-endorsing in virtual environments. *Journal of Advertising, 40*(2), 93–106. https://doi.org/10.2753/JOA0091-3367400207

Anderson, E. W. (1998). Customer satisfaction and word of mouth. *Journal of Service Research, 1*(1), 5–17. https://doi.org/10.1177/109467059800100102

Arndt, J. (1967). Role of product-related conversations in the diffusion of a new product. *Journal of Marketing Research, 4*(3), 291. https://doi.org/10.2307/3149462

Bigné, J. E., Sánchez, M. I., & Sánchez, J. (2001). Tourism image, evaluation variables and after purchase behaviour: Inter-relationship. *Tourism Management, 22*(6), 607–616. https://doi.org/10.1016/S0261-5177(01)00035-8

Brewer, J., & Dourish, P. (2008). Storied spaces: Cultural accounts of mobility, technology, and environmental knowing. *International Journal of Human-Computer Studies, 66*(12), 963–976. https://doi.org/10.1016/j.ijhcs.2008.03.003

Buzova, D., Cervera-Taulet, A., & Sanz-Blas, S. (2020). Exploring multisensory place experiences through cruise blog analysis. *Psychology & Marketing, 37*(1), 131–140. https://doi.org/10.1002/mar.21286

Casey, E. S. (2001). On Habitus and place: Responding to my critics. *Annals of the Association of American Geographers, 91*(4), 716–723. https://doi.org/10.1111/0004-5608.00270

Chen, Z., Cenfetelli, R., & Benbasat, I. (2019). *The influence of e-commerce live streaming on lifestyle fit uncertainty and online purchase intention of experience products*. Hawaii International Conference on System Sciences. https://doi.org/10.24251/HICSS.2019.610

Cheng, A. S., Kruger, L. E., & Daniels, S. E. (2003). 'Place' as an integrating concept in natural resource politics: Propositions for a social science research agenda. *Society & Natural Resources, 16*(2), 87–104. https://doi.org/10.1080/08941920309199

Ciolfi, L. (2004). *Situating "place" in interaction design: Enhancing the user experience in interactive environments*. University of Limerick (Ireland).

Cohen, E. (1972). Towards a sociology of international tourism. *Social Research: An International Quarterly, 39*, 164–189.

Cohen, E. (1979). Rethinking the sociology of tourism. *Annals of Tourism Research, 6*(1), 18–35. https://doi.org/10.1016/0160-7383(79)90092-6

Connell, J., & Gibson, C. (2004). Vicarious journeys: Travels in music. *Tourism Geographies, 6*(1), 2–25. https://doi.org/10.1080/1461668032000172319

Dahl, S., Eagle, L., & Báez, C. (2009). Analyzing advergames: Active diversions or actually deception. An exploratory study of online advergames content. *Young Consumers, 10*(1), 46–59. https://doi.org/10.1108/17473610910940783

Dann, G., & Jacobsen, J. K. S. (2003). Tourism smellscapes. *Tourism Geographies, 5*(1), 3–25. https://doi.org/10.1080/1461668032000034033

Dann, G. M. S., & Jacobsen, J. K. S. (2002). Leading the tourist by the nose. In G. M. S. Dann (Ed.), *The tourist as a metaphor of the social world* (pp. 209–235). CABI. https://doi.org/10.1079/9780851996066.0209

Edensor, T. (2006). Sensing tourist spaces. In C. Minca & T. Oakes (Eds.), *Travels in paradox: Remapping tourism* (pp. 23–35). Rowman & Littlefield.

Fazio, R. H., & Zanna, M. P. (1978). Attitudinal qualities relating to the strength of the attitude-behavior relationship. *Journal of Experimental Social Psychology, 14*(4), 398–408. https://doi.org/10.1016/0022-1031(78)90035-5

Franklin, A., & Crang, M. (2001). The trouble with tourism and travel theory? *Tourist Studies, 1*(1), 5–22. https://doi.org/10.1177/146879760 100100101

Giuliani, M. V., & Feldman, R. (1993). Place attachment in a developmental and cultural context. *Journal of Environmental Psychology, 13*(3), 267–274. https://doi.org/10.1016/S0272-4944(05)80179-3

Goh, K.-Y., Ping, J., & National University of Singapore. (2014). Engaging consumers with advergames: An experimental evaluation of interactivity, fit and expectancy. *Journal of the Association for Information Systems, 15*(7), 388–421. https://doi.org/10.17705/1jais.00366

Govers, R., & Go, F. M. (2005). Projected destination image online: Website content analysis of pictures and text. *Information Technology & Tourism, 7*(2), 73–89. https://doi.org/10.3727/1098305054517327

Govers, R., Go, F. M., & Kumar, K. (2007). Virtual destination image a new measurement approach. *Annals of Tourism Research, 34*(4), 977–997. https://doi.org/10.1016/j.annals.2007.06.001

Griffith, D. A., & Chen, Q. (2004). The influence of virtual direct experience (vde) on on-line ad message effectiveness. *Journal of Advertising, 33*(1), 55–68. https://doi.org/10.1080/00913367.2004.10639153

Gustafson, P. (2001). Meanings of place: Everyday experience and theoretical conceptualizations. *Journal of Environmental Psychology, 21*(1), 5–16. https://doi.org/10.1006/jevp.2000.0185

Harrison, S., & Dourish, P. (1996). Re-place-ing space: The roles of place and space in collaborative systems. *Proceedings of the 1996 ACM Conference on Computer Supported Cooperative Work —CSCW '96,* 67–76. https://doi.org/10.1145/240080.240193

Hidalgo, M. C., & Hernández, B. (2001). Place attachment: Conceptual and empirical questions. *Journal of Environmental Psychology, 21*(3), 273–281. https://doi.org/10.1006/jevp.2001.0221

Hirschman, E. C., & Holbrook, M. B. (1982). Hedonic consumption: Emerging concepts, methods and propositions. *Journal of Marketing, 46*(3), 92. https://doi.org/10.2307/1251707

Hirschman, E. C., & Holbrook, M. B. (1986). Expanding the ontology and methodology of research on the consumption experience. In D. Brinberg & R. J. Lutz (Eds.), *Perspectives on methodology in consumer research* (pp. 213–251). Springer. https://doi.org/10.1007/978-1-4613-8609-4_7

Holbrook, M. B., & Hirschman, E. C. (1982). The experiential aspects of consumption: Consumer fantasies, feelings, and fun. *Journal of Consumer Research, 9*(2), 132. https://doi.org/10.1086/208906

Jaakson, R. (1986). Second-home domestic tourism. *Annals of Tourism Research, 13*(3), 367–391. https://doi.org/10.1016/0160-7383(86)90026-5

Jiang, Z., & Benbasat, I. (2004). Virtual product experience: Effects of visual and functional control of products on perceived diagnosticity and flow in electronic shopping. *Journal of Management Information Systems, 21*(3), 111–147. https://doi.org/10.1080/07421222.2004.11045817

Jiang, Z., & Benbasat, I. (2007). The effects of presentation formats and task complexity on online consumers' product understanding. *MIS Quarterly, 31*(3), 475. https://doi.org/10.2307/25148804

Jones, M. A., Reynolds, K. E., & Arnold, M. J. (2006). Hedonic and utilitarian shopping value: Investigating differential effects on retail outcomes. *Journal of Business Research, 59*(9), 974–981. https://doi.org/10.1016/j.jbusres.2006.03.006

Kaltenborn, B. P. (1998). Effects of sense of place on responses to environmental impacts. *Applied Geography, 18*(2), 169–189. https://doi.org/10.1016/S0143-6228(98)00002-2

Kim, H., & Richardson, S. L. (2003). Motion picture impacts on destination images. *Annals of Tourism Research, 30*(1), 216–237. https://doi.org/10.1016/S0160-7383(02)00062-2

Kim, Y. M., & Shim, K. (2002). The influence of internet shopping mall characteristics and user traits on purchase intent. *Irish Marketing Review, 15*(2), 25–34.

Kyle, G., & Chick, G. (2007). The social construction of a sense of place. *Leisure Sciences, 29*(3), 209–225.

Lau, K. W., Lee, P. Y., & Lau, H. F. (2014). Shopping experience 2.0: An exploration of how consumers are shopping in an immersive virtual reality. *Advances in Economics and Business, 2*(2), 92–99.

Lentini, L., & Decortis, F. (2010). Space and places: When interacting with and in physical space becomes a meaningful experience. *Personal and Ubiquitous Computing, 14*, 407–415.

Lew, A. (1999). Editorial: Tourism enclaves in place and mind. *Tourism Geographies, 6*(1), 1–1. https://doi.org/10.1080/1461668032000172283

Li, H., Daugherty, T., & Biocca, F. (2002). Impact of 3-d advertising on product knowledge, brand attitude, and purchase intention: The Mediating role of presence. *Journal of Advertising, 31*(3), 43–57. https://doi.org/10.1080/00913367.2002.10673675

Li, H., Daugherty, T., & Biocca, F. (2003). The role of virtual experience in consumer learning. *Journal of Consumer Psychology, 13*(4), 395–407. https://doi.org/10.1207/S15327663JCP1304_07

Li, Y. (2000). Geographical consciousness and tourism experience. *Annals of Tourism Research, 27*(4), 863–883. https://doi.org/10.1016/S0160-7383(99)00112-7

Mannell, R. C., & Iso-Ahola, S. E. (1987). Psychological nature of leisure and tourism experience. *Annals of Tourism Research, 14*(3), 314–331. https://doi.org/10.1016/0160-7383(87)90105-8

Maxham, J. G. (2001). Service recovery's influence on consumer satisfaction, positive word-of-mouth, and purchase intentions. *Journal of Business Research, 54*(1), 11–24. https://doi.org/10.1016/S0148-2963(00)00114-4

McCarthy, J., & Wright, P. (2005). Technology in place: Dialogics of technology, place and self. In M. F. Costabile & F. Paternò (Eds.), *Human-computer interaction—Interact 2005* (Vol. 3585, pp. 914–926). Springer. https://doi.org/10.1007/11555261_72

Meyrowitz, J. (1986). *No sense of place: The impact of electronic media on social behavior* (1. issued as an Oxford Univ. Press paperback). Oxford University Press.

Mingers, J. (2001). Embodying information systems: The contribution of phenomenology. *Information and Organization, 11*(2), 103–128. https://doi.org/10.1016/S1471-7727(00)00005-1

Murphy, P., Pritchard, M. P., & Smith, B. (2000). The destination product and its impact on traveller perceptions. *Tourism Management, 21*(1), 43–52. https://doi.org/10.1016/S0261-5177(99)00080-1

Pearce, P. L. (1991). Analysing tourist attractions. *Journal of Tourism Studies, 2*(1), 46–55.

Pham, M. T. (1998). Representativeness, relevance, and the use of feelings in decision making. *Journal of Consumer Research, 25*(2), 144–159. https://doi.org/10.1086/209532

Ping, J. W., Goh, K. Y., & Teo, H. H. (2010). Engaging consumers with advergames: An experimental evaluation of interactivity, relevance and expectancy. In *Proceedings of the 31th international conference on information systems*. Saint Louis, Missouri, December 12–15, 2010, Paper 221: 1–21.

Raymond, C. M., Kyttä, M., & Stedman, R. (2017). Sense of place, fast and slow: The potential contributions of affordance theory to sense of place. *Frontiers in Psychology, 8*, 1674. https://doi.org/10.3389/fpsyg.2017.01674

Relph, E. (1976). *Place and placelessness*. Sage.

Richins, M. L. (1983). Negative word-of-mouth by dissatisfied consumers: A pilot study. *Journal of Marketing, 47*(1), 68. https://doi.org/10.2307/3203428

Rickly-Boyd, J. M. (2009). The tourist narrative. *Tourist Studies, 9*(3), 259–280. https://doi.org/10.1177/1468797610382701

Ryan, C. (2010). Ways of conceptualizing the tourist experience a review of literature. *Tourism Recreation Research*, 35(1), 37–46. https://doi.org/10.1080/02508281.2010.11081617

Sack, R. D. (1992). *Place, modernity and the consumer's world*. The Johns Hopkins University Press.

Schmäh, M., Wilke, T., & Rossmann, A. (2017, December). Electronic word-of-mouth: A systematic literature analysis. In A. Rossmann & A. Zimmermann (Eds.), *Digital enterprise computing* (pp. 147–158). Gesellschaft für Informatik.

Seamon, D. (1982). The phenomenological contribution to environmental psychology. *Journal of Environmental Psychology*, 2(2), 119–140. https://doi.org/10.1016/S0272-4944(82)80044-3

Seamon, D. (2018). Merleau-Ponty, lived body, and place: Toward a phenomenology of human situatedness. In T. Hünefeldt & A. Schlitte (Eds.), *Situatedness and place* (Vol. 95, pp. 41–66). Springer. https://doi.org/10.1007/978-3-319-92937-8_4

Shamai, S. (1991). Sense of place: An empirical measurement. *Geoforum*, 22(3), 347–358. https://doi.org/10.1016/0016-7185(91)90017-K

Shiv, B., & Fedorikhin, A. (1999). Heart and mind in conflict: The interplay of affect and cognition in consumer decision making. *Journal of Consumer Research*, 26(3), 278–292. https://doi.org/10.1086/209563

Simpson, P. M., & Siguaw, J. A. (2008). Destination word of mouth: The role of traveler type, residents, and identity salience. *Journal of Travel Research*, 47(2), 167–182. https://doi.org/10.1177/0047287508321198

Singh, J. (1988). Consumer complaint intentions and behavior: Definitional and taxonomical issues. *Journal of Marketing*, 52(1), 93. https://doi.org/10.2307/1251688

Smyth, M., Benyon, D., McCall, R., O'Neill, S., & Carroll, F. (2015). Patterns of place: An integrated approach for the design and evaluation of real and virtual environments. In M. Lombard, F. Biocca, J. Freeman, W. IJsselsteijn, & R. J. Schaevitz (Eds.), *Immersed in media* (pp. 237–260). Springer. https://doi.org/10.1007/978-3-319-10190-3_10

Snepenger, D., Murphy, L., Snepenger, M., & Anderson, W. (2004). Normative meanings of experiences for a spectrum of tourism places. *Journal of Travel Research*, 43(2), 108–117. https://doi.org/10.1177/0047287504268231

Snepenger, D., Snepenger, M., Dalbey, M., & Wessol, A. (2007). Meanings and consumption characteristics of places at a tourism destination. *Journal of Travel Research*, 45(3), 310–321. https://doi.org/10.1177/0047287506295909

Spielmann, N., Babin, B. J., & Manthiou, A. (2018). Places as authentic consumption contexts. *Psychology & Marketing*, 35(9), 652–665. https://doi.org/10.1002/mar.21113

Stedman, R. C. (2006). Understanding place attachment among second home owners. *American Behavioral Scientist, 50*(2), 187–205. https://doi.org/10.1177/0002764206290633

Suh, K.-S., & Chang, S. (2006). User interfaces and consumer perceptions of online stores: The role of telepresence. *Behaviour & Information Technology, 25*(2), 99–113. https://doi.org/10.1080/01449290500330398

Taylor, S. E., & Thompson, S. C. (1982). Stalking the elusive 'vividness' effect. *Psychological Review, 89*(2), 155–181. https://doi.org/10.1037/0033-295X.89.2.155

Tjostheim, I. (2020). *Experiencing sense of place in a virtual environment: Real in the moment?* [Report RR-20.02]. Umeå Universitet.

Tribe, J., & Xiao, H. (2011). Developments in tourism social science. *Annals of Tourism Research, 38*(1), 7–26. https://doi.org/10.1016/j.annals.2010.11.012

Turner, P., & Turner, S. (2006). Place, sense of place, and presence. *Presence: Teleoperators and Virtual Environments, 15*(2), 204–217. https://doi.org/10.1162/pres.2006.15.2.204

Turner, P., Turner, S., & Carroll, F. (2005). The tourist gaze: Towards contextualised virtual environments. *Spaces, spatiality and technology* (pp. 281–297). Kluwer Springer.

Vogt, C. A., & Fesenmaier, D. R. (1998). Expanding the functional information search model. *Annals of Tourism Research, 25*(3), 551–578. https://doi.org/10.1016/S0160-7383(98)00010-3

Williams, D. R., & Kaltenborn, B. P. (1999). Leisure places and modernity: The use and meaning of recreational cottages in Norway and the USA. In D. Crouch (Ed.), *Leisure/tourism geographies: Practices and geographical knowledge* (pp. 214–230). Routledge.

Williams, D. R., Patterson, M. E., Roggenbuck, J. W., & Watson, A. E. (1992). Beyond the commodity metaphor: Examining emotional and symbolic attachment to place. *Leisure Sciences, 14*(1), 29–46. https://doi.org/10.1080/01490409209513155

Williams, D. R., & Vaske, J. J. (2003). The measurement of place attachment: Validity and generalizability of a psychometric approach. *Forest Science, 49*(6), 830–840.

Wu, C., & Shaffer, D. R. (1987). Susceptibility to persuasive appeals as a function of source credibility and prior experience with the attitude object. *Journal of Personality and Social Psychology, 52*(4), 677–688. https://doi.org/10.1037/0022-3514.52.4.677

Yu, Y., & Dean, A. (2001). The contribution of emotional satisfaction to consumer loyalty. *International Journal of Service Industry Management, 12*(3), 234–250. https://doi.org/10.1108/09564230110393239

Open Access This chapter is licensed under the terms of the Creative Commons Attribution 4.0 International License (http://creativecommons.org/licenses/by/4.0/), which permits use, sharing, adaptation, distribution and reproduction in any medium or format, as long as you give appropriate credit to the original author(s) and the source, provide a link to the Creative Commons license and indicate if changes were made.

The images or other third party material in this chapter are included in the chapter's Creative Commons license, unless indicated otherwise in a credit line to the material. If material is not included in the chapter's Creative Commons license and your intended use is not permitted by statutory regulation or exceeds the permitted use, you will need to obtain permission directly from the copyright holder.

CHAPTER 5

The Reality of Digital Travel

Abstract It is the experience that counts, there and then. When a person talks about the experience, he or she can also reflect on and interpret the experience. In this chapter we use findings from empirical studies and surveys to write about the subjective reality of digital travel. We discussed the theoretical foundation for why we can have the feeling of being there (and what we referred to as the Spinozan model of perception) in Chapters 2 and 3. The first studies we report are on factors affecting the sense of place experience, and telepresence, using video games to create a sightseeing environment for participants. The second study is a survey of citizens on the topic of vacation planning, digital travel applications before, during and after visiting a tourist destination.

Keywords Surveys · Digital sightseeing · Travel apps · Sense of place

INTRODUCTION

In this chapter, we look at the factors affecting digital travel. We present cases and review experimental results from studies comparing various rated aspects of the telepresence experience and the sense of place in realistic virtual settings. We look at situations in which the place experience is evoked by new technologies, and present results suggesting that there are valid reasons for building on previous telepresence research, and using some existing scales or measurements from the telepresence field. We then outline how concepts from human geography and marketing, such as word-of-mouth recommendation, intention to visit and perceptible affordance, can also be important.

We identify which of the various components that can contribute to telepresence are most important, for example, perceptual realism and its relation to sensory experiences in virtual environments, relating this back to our earlier discussions of the psychological and philosophical underpinnings of the sense of presence in Chapter 3. We examine how this relates to sense of place, using our own expanded version of Relph's multi-component model of the elements of sense of place we described in Chapter 4. We also look at the dimension of hedonistic consumption, from marketing research, since this can be seen as an important factor in the motivation to undertake virtual travel and meetings.

Concerning the current status of digital travel, we share findings from a recent survey of vacation planning among people from Norway, in the summer of 2021. The backdrop is the pandemic situation with restrictions on travel. Although Norway is one of the least effected countries in terms of numbers infected, patients in hospitals and deaths due to the COVID-19 virus, the national health authorities and the government have recommended citizens not to travel abroad or to places in the country with outbreaks of COVID-19. Due to the progress of vaccination, with 50% of the population 16 years of older with at least one vaccination-dose at the time of writing, many of the restrictions, for instance, 10 days in quarantine hotel after a travel abroad, have been taken away for the fully vaccinated. For those with one dose, it is currently only a 3-day stay at home quarantine after travel abroad, unless a test at the border shows that a traveller has the virus. Moreover, since most countries in Europe have open borders for travellers with a negative virus test or a vaccination certificate, many have started their vacation planning or have decided to travel. The survey results should be interpreted in this context.

Because the topic is virtual tourism, digital travel and the future of travel, it is significant that the citizens have had a year and a half with few opportunities for travelling abroad. Although most of the restrictions have been accepted by the population, the longer the pandemic has lasted more people have felt a need for a normal vacation. For many in Norway, this means a holiday in Europe, in particular to the Mediterranean region.

Because of this, the question of digital travel as a substitute for actual travel is not an unreasonable or purely theoretical question but rather a timely one in the context of actual travel planning.

The chapter has also a theoretical focus. For empirical research, the choice of methods and measurements matter. For instance, there are some limitations that have to do with the participants' willingness to answer a survey or to take part in a video game study in person. For researchers, there are always alternatives that demand methodological choices. Of the two studies presented in this chapter, the video game study was the more time-consuming and focused study while the digital travel study has less depth, but could be carried out in a specific situation just before the main holiday-season in Norway. For both studies the term "travel experience" plays a key role. For the survey, the broader perspective, we are influenced by and build on the works of Erik Cohen for a way to describe travel motives and modes of tourism experiences.

In tourism research, Cohen is one of the most influential scholars. In his 1979 paper on the nature of the tourism experience he distinguishes between five main modes of tourism experience. In Cohen's paper there are no references to telepresence or digital travel, but this is not to say that the five modes cannot be applied in this context. We find the first two, recreational and diversionary modes, particularly relevant for digital travel. These two modes concern entertainment, breaking out of daily routines and stress. They can also be used to describe to the extent to which an experience in a digital environment is a recreational or diversionary tourism experience.

Finally, there are opportunities created by technology. Due to the pandemic, digital meetings are not extraordinary, but rather common in work life and more generally. Similarly, visits to museum, broadcasted digital concerts and cultural events are actual alternatives for many to visiting in person. The pandemic had an immediate effect on the travel and hospitality industry, events, cultural institutions and the service sectors related to these industries. Due to the many restrictions, and the fact that it has not been possible to predict when the pandemic will be over, companies in these industries have looked for alternatives. Examples are the news story by skift.com, 1 April 2020 *"Tour Guides and Attractions Operators Shift to Testing Experiences – Online"*, 9 March 2021

"Heritage Sites Copy Tricks from Video Games to Woo Visitors[1]" and the company Eventbrite' future outlook, 26 March 2021:

> When we looked at the year-over-year data comparing March 2020 to March 2021, virtual tour and virtual travel events increased a staggering 41X. Although this growth will likely taper off as we start safely gathering in-person again, virtual travel and virtual tours have enabled people around the globe to experience new places from the comfort of their couches, and have given people access to places they perhaps could never travel to in person, and that's a trend we hope continues post-pandemic.

The digital travel survey that we present in the second section of this chapter contains information on the current situation in the use of digital travel apps and virtual presentations.

Digital Travel and Sense of Place

In this section we present findings from an empirical study of a digital visit to Los Angeles in a video game. But first we ask: what is the relationship of a visit to a place in VE and an experience in vivo? The prerequisite for this question is that the VE used in the video game study is a replication of an actual place, the city of Los Angeles. Secondly, and particularly relevant for tourists on vacation, what is it that the person (traveller, tourist) would like to do in a virtual environment?

In Chapter 2 we presented Gibson's affordance concept. Affordances are about action, intention to behave or actual behaviour. It is a useful concept theoretically as well as practically (method-wise). Few studies have compared the virtual actions with actual behaviour in the material world (Burke et al., 1992; Clemenson et al., 2020; Khenak et al., 2020; Mania & Chalmers, 2001; Nisenfeld 2003; Tjostheim & Haugland, 2005; Tjostheim & Saether-Larsen, 2005; Usoh et al., 2000). The results from these studies indicate that there are correlations and many similarities between the two. However, it is not an easy task to design an empirical study to investigate this relationship (Howlett et al., 2005). In the Howlett study the respective times taken to complete tasks in the

---

[1] Questo has invented games for tourists to play in more than 80 cities via its mobile app. Players can pretend to explore cities in the guise of major figures, such as travelling around Zurich as Einstein, and listen to stories about local history in exchange for earning points in a game (Skift.com, October 19, 2020).

real and virtual worlds were compared in order to establish how well the virtual experience mimicked the real-world scenario.

To study digital travel and sense of place we chose a city well known to many tourists, Los Angeles. Sightseeing is a popular activity, particularly for tourists (Adler, 1989; Dunn-Ross & Iso-Ahola, 1991). It is not something all travellers do, but it is rarely necessary to explain what it is. Sightseeing is meaningful in a virtual environment of a city as well as when actually visiting the city in vivo. This was a prerequisite for the study. Some researchers use the term ecological validity when they discuss this question—the goal is that the findings are representative, meaningful outside the study-context. Also, city tourism is particularly common among young travellers, which is relevant because we recruited students as our study participants.

THE USE OF VIDEO GAMES AND PHOTO-REALISM

It is not difficult to find virtual environments of cities because in a number of video games the setting for the story is an urban environment or a place with which the player is quite likely to be familiar. The Xbox game *Project Gotham Racing 4* (*PGR4*) can serve as illustration. In this game the player drives a car in the streets of London, Macau, Las Vegas, St Petersburg, Tokyo, New York City, Shanghai and Quebec. There is a second reason for mentioning this game; in *PGR4* there is also an alternative to the racing option, called "*tourist mode*", in which the player can explore the cities in the game without competing. There are other examples, such as the Playstation game *Gangs of London* that also features a tourist mode. In the tourist mode the player can explore and take photographs of the city's most famous landmarks. The most recent game by Xbox at the time of writing, Forza Horizon 5, launched in November 2021, features places in Mexico including the city of Guanajuato.

Widyarto and Latiff (2007) argue that a virtual application works well in a travel context as a tool for getting to know the place, for instance, for navigation purposes. Schwartz (2006), in his study of video games, discusses the fact that many games combine fantasy with a sense of realism. He uses the game *Grand Theft Auto* as an example and cites a player who says: "*you feel as if you're in a real town/city with other people*" (Schwartz, 2006: 315). According to Schwartz (2006), realism and attention to detail allow gamers to accept the game spaces as real, and therefore some gamers choose to visit the game space, that is, they explore the game space as a tourist would explore a physical location.

There are several genres of video game, one of which is termed *"life simulations"* (Jong et al., 2013). For life simulations, the goal is not to mimic social interaction as accurately as possible, but often, social interaction plays a role. There is also a trend referred to as *"realism"* (Dormans, 2011), which might explain why the graphics in many games are often based on photography. There is a second aspect to realism in games. As Sommerseth (2007: 767) argues that: *"realism is dependent on actions rendering expected results in a game. The question of realism is tied to the experience of the player, rather than the constructed environment of the game"*.

A study by Gackenbach and Bown (2011) concerned video games in different genres: action, adventure, driving, miscellaneous, roleplaying and sports. They used the Temple Presence Inventory (Lombard et al., 2009) to measure perceptual richness. One of the conclusions was that perceptual richness, *"which is about how the game is like the real world"*, has a positive impact particularly for sport, but also for action games. In a fantasy world, it is not important to replicate a city or another place that can be visited. However, in a tourism context and with sightseeing in a city as the activity, realism is obviously important. The VE of the city should be, and be perceived as, similar to the actual city. Then it makes sense to study tourist behaviour in the VE.

We used the video game *Midnight Club LA*, a Playstation game, to study sense of place. The choice of the video game with the city Los Angeles was primarily based on the following two factors; (1) realism and (2) the fact that many users know how to navigate in a game environment. Not all citizens are experienced video gamers, but most people know the basics, how games work. Often with IT applications there is a learning phase before the user can concentrate on doing what he or she is supposed to do. To move forward in the game environment, to stop, etc. To race fast might require some skills, but the younger generation often have these skills already. For the sightseeing in the Los Angeles study, only very basic video game skills were needed. The level of realism is high in the game, mostly because of the attention to detail and good graphics made by the developers of the game.

The game *Driver: San Francisco* by Ubisoft has many similarities to *Midnight club LA*. This is a review of this game by Joe Barron[2]:

> Driver: San Francisco is, as you might have already guessed, set in the real-world San Francisco, as well as small parts of Marin County and Oakland. All in all, there will be a staggering 208 miles of road, all of which is looking remarkably detailed in what has been shown of the game so far. The graphical detail and the rock solid 60 frames per second are very impressive for a game of this scale. The environments look superb, if a little stylized, and the city's landmarks are instantly recognizable. Roads are populated with far more traffic than we are used to seeing in other open-world games and all of the cars are very well modelled with detailed textures which would not look out of place in closed-circuit racing games like Forza Motorsport and Shift. All of this detail combined with such a superb frame-rate should make this version of San Francisco one of the most accurate and enjoyable yet seen in games.

The trend towards convergences between gaming and cinema, and gaming and online technologies, started at least 15 years ago (Freitas & Griffiths, 2008). The key aspect is realism. One technique to achieve realism is to merge computer-generated graphics with real-life images. For a normal viewer it is sometimes impossible to distinguish between a photorealistic computer image and a photographic image (Lyu & Farid, 2005; Maejima et al., 2010). An example from the film-industry is the science-fiction thriller "*Alita: Battle Angel*" by Robert Rodriguez and James Cameron, released in January 2019. In many scenes in this movie CGI animation is combined with live action. For most viewers it is hard to distinguish between graphics and film in the action scenes.

CREATING A SIGHTSEEING EXPERIENCE IN A VIDEO GAME

Photo-realism matters, but it is not only the visual aspects that plays a role in a sense of place experience. In the Los Angeles study, the activity given to the participants was sightseeing in a famous area in the city. Often there is a guide telling the tourist, the sightseer, what he or she is looking at, and stories about the place. There are many good reasons for this, one being that people think narratively (Weick, 1995; Woodside et al.,

---

[2] http://www.hookedgamers.com/pc/driver_san_francisco/preview/article-890.html.

2007). There is an entertainment element to it also—good stories are persuasive (McKee, 2003; Woodside & Megehee, 2010). Turner et al. (2005) comment that the users of a virtual environment need a meaningful narrative in order to create an engaging experience and a sense of place. A sightseeing experience in a VE is more than a visual experience. Narratives are, for example, stories that a user can inhabit from a first-person perspective. The narrative creates meaning for the individual's experience in a virtual environment. The narrative plot can be an important contributor to the sense of being there (Gorini et al., 2011; Turner et al., 2013).

Some tourists go sightseeing on their own without a guide present. There is also the possibility of using an audio guide that can be played on a mobile device, for instance, a mobile phone. We chose this alternative. For the city Los Angeles, we chose audio guides that the traveller can use while visiting the area that includes Hollywood Boulevard. The narrative for the sightseeing tour was made from a Tourcaster audio guide, a guide that can be downloaded on a mobile phone or another device. In vivo a tourist will turn the audio guide on and off himself, and listen when it suits him. For this study, we had to produce a narrative that was the same for all participants.

The sightseeing was a live event in the sense that the visuals of the game were used without any adaptation. In order to create a better sightseeing experience, the music that comes as a component of the game was turned off and replaced by an audio clip taken from the Tourcaster *"Hollywood Audio Tour"*. The audio came from a laptop computer placed in front of the participant, the sightseer. No information was given regarding the name of the Playstation game. In the next section we give more details about the design of the study.

A Virtual Visit to Los Angeles

The game *Midnight Club LA* features some of the well-known sections of the city Los Angeles. With the game and an audio guide, we designed a sightseeing tour in the city, in Hollywood Boulevard and the historic district, a live event that lasted approximately 15 minutes. The guide told stories about the buildings, events, movies and what the person could see when he or she is actually there in the streets.

In the game, the player can drive on the road or on the pavement, but not through buildings. Similarly, the tourist, the participant in the study could freely navigate in Los Angeles in the game. Because we framed the event as a sightseeing tour, the participant had to follow instructions from the guide (recorded in advance) and also instructions by the interviewer as a co-guide. The participant, the sightseer was only given instructions if she moved too fast or too slowly. The setting was an auditorium with a big screen—the Playstation console was connected to a monitor.

A total of 60 individuals, primarily students participated in the LA study, from a number of countries. Of the 60 participants, 60% were female and 40% were male, 48% were between 19 and 24 years of age, and 75% answered that they used video or computer games approximately once a month or less frequently. The nationalities of the 19 summer school students were; Azerbaijan, Bangladesh, China, Croatia, Ethiopia, Greece, Kosovo, Lithuania, Nepal, Pakistan, Portugal, Tanzania, Ukraine, USA and Zimbabwe. The other 41 students came from Norway.

The Sightseers' Experience of Telepresence and Sense of Place

To measure the telepresence experience, it is common to use questions that distinguish between aspects that constitute telepresence. The measurement, the Temple Presence Inventory (TPI) by Lombard et al. (2000, 2009, 2011) has these factors: engagement (mental immersion), spatial presence, social realism, social presence and perceptual realness. For the Los Angeles study, the participants answered questions for each for these factors on a seven-point Likert scale from fully disagree to fully agree.

Relph's place theory (Relph, 1976) has been used for numerous studies of sense of place, or experience of place (e.g. Benyon et al., 2006; Seamon, 1982, 1996, 2000, 2018; Shamai, 1991; Smith, 2006; Smyth et al., 2015; Turner & Turner, 2006; Turner et al., 2005). Traditionally, human geography has not been concerned with virtual reality, and the role of technology. Researchers in this field have primarily focused on humans living in a place, on secondary homeowners, and less frequently on visitors to the place. Edward Relph has a phenomenological perspective in his work. He discusses everyday experiences and the relationship between the human and the place. In the introduction to his paper "*Spirit of Place and Sense of Place in Virtual Realities*" (2007) Edward Relph comments on place and VR:

I have written about the concept "place" from a phenomenological perspective for many years…, but we have limited knowledge of digital virtual reality… Nevertheless, it seems to me that mutual interaction is at work between what might be called "real" place and virtual places." His view reflects the notion that virtual places cannot be authentic, but "virtual places can be more or less accurate reproductions (our emphasis) of real places and more or less convincing on their own terms. (Relph, 2007: 23)

In Chapter 4 (Table 4.1) we presented the two main categories; insideness sense of place and outsideness sense of place with four and three types, seven in total. Relph distinguishes between these seven types of place experience, but they are not all possible variants for tourists. In comparison with residents, tourists visit a place for a short time. Hence, the outsideness categories seem to be the most appropriate for tourism and a sightseeing experience.

We could not find any that had developed a measurement based on Relph's experience of place theory. We therefore decided to develop a measurement that included behavioural outsideness and vicarious outsideness (unpublished thesis, Tjostheim, 2020), two new types in addition to the seven by Relph in *Place and Placelessness* (Relph, 1976), as discussed in Chapter 4. For the Los Angeles study we used a measurement, a questionnaire with statements similar in form to the Temple Presence Inventory. Shamai (1991: 349) writes that: "Each different way of sensing the place can be seen as a different level on an ordinal scale; that is, starting with the lowest level of sense of place and 'climbing' up six more steps to reach the most intense and deepest way of sensing a place". See Table 4.3, in Chapter 4, for a description of these two additional types of placeness, behavioural outsideness and vicarious outsideness, and how they relate to the seven types identified by Relph (1976).

In the survey, the participants also answered questions about how knowledgeable they considered themselves to be about Los Angeles and whether they had been to Los Angeles. Knowledge of the destination was measured with a three-item scale adapted from Smith and Park (1992) and Suh and Chang (2006). The purpose was to have a scale that could be used before and after the sightseeing in the VE, to observe the immediate effect of the experience in the VE.

Los Angeles is a tourist destination. In the survey, we included a question about intention to visit the city the next three years. Is this intention related to actual behaviour? In consumer studies purchase intention is often used as a measure of anticipated response behaviour (Bearden et al., 1984). According to Tian-Cole and Crompton (2003), a person's intention to visit a destination is a determinant of their actual behaviour of visiting that destination or not. Hence a question about behavioural intentions can be used as a surrogate for a destination choice.

Results—Virtual Sightseers Had the Feeling of Being There in the City

Our main interest was to investigate whether or not the digital sightseer had the feeling of *being there*, and what type of sense of place experience the sightseer had. Figure 5.1 shows the scores measured on a scale of 1–7.

Figure 5.1 shows on average a score on the positive side of the scale for all three concepts, telepresence, sense of place and the hedonic consumption experience. When there are significant differences in the variances in the answers, as in this case, the average score does not give the best information. We therefore show three groups (Fig. 5.2). The first is those that answered 1–3, referred to as the negative group for telepresence, those that did not have the feeling of being there. The second group is

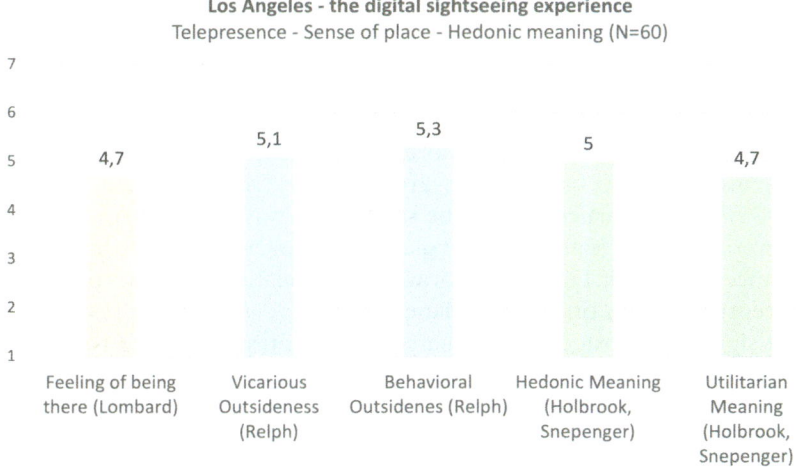

Fig. 5.1 How the participants experienced Los Angeles measured with three alternative measurements

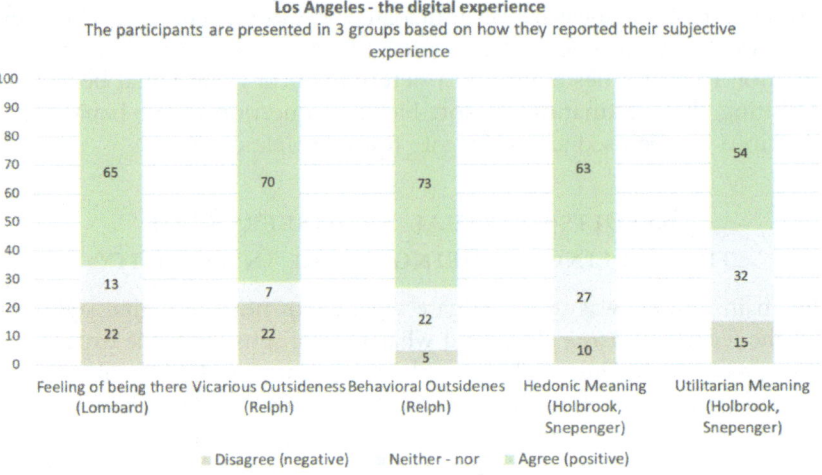

Fig. 5.2 Los Angeles—the feeling of being there

the neither-nor group, those that answered 4. The third group consists of those that did experience the feeling of being there, and similarly for sense of place and hedonic consumption experience.

The main finding was that 2 out of 3 participants reported a feeling of being there, a sense of place experience and/or a hedonic consumption experience (Fig. 5.2). The participants were asked to report how they felt, and the interviews took place immediately after the digital sightseeing.

The questions in the Temple Presence Inventory about perceptual realism were used to create three groups. The "senses evoked group" were 18 of the 60 participants in the study. This was the 18 that reported that several of their senses were evoked. We looked at the score on the affordances question. Figure 5.3 shows the correlation with, or the effect of perceptual realism on the affordances.

The sightseeing lasted approximately 15 minutes Compared to TV or online advertisements this is a long time. It is also an interactive experience and not only a viewing experience. Could we see a direct effect of the digital sightseeing experience on the participants? The questionnaire before and the after-the-sightseeing questionnaire had these three questions:

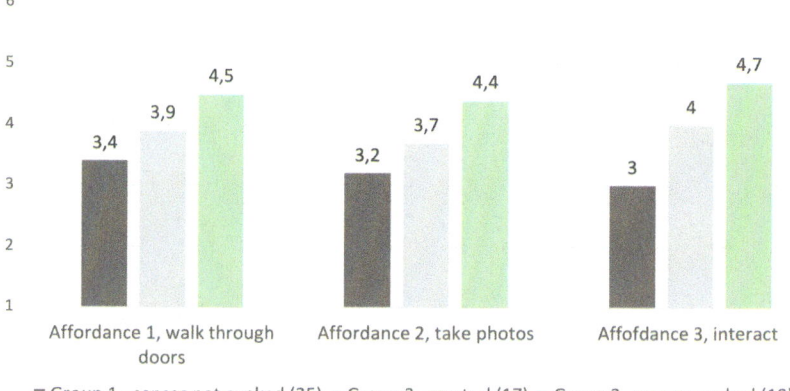

Fig. 5.3 Los Angeles—perceptual realism and affordances

(a) "As a tourist destination I feel very knowledgeable about Los Angeles"
(b) "I feel if I had to book a trip to Los Angeles today, I would need to gather very little information in order to make a wise decision"
(c) "I feel very confident of my ability to judge the quality of a trip to this city"

The answers to these questions indicated that the digital experience had a direct impact on the participants—see Fig. 5.4.

Readers of human geography know the works of Edward Relph, especially his place theory. How Relph describes sense of place is well known to researchers in human geography. In tourism, his place theory is known, but not very often incorporated or used by tourism scholars. Based on our Los Angeles study, we would argue that it seems quite appropriate to apply the place theory of Edward Relph to digital experiences as well as for actual visits by travellers to tourist destinations.

The "hosts" at actual tourist destinations consist of many groups; from professional service employees in the tourism and hospitality industry to locals that only occasionally interact directly with visitors. It is not likely that a city, a town or a small place without any locals will be an attractive

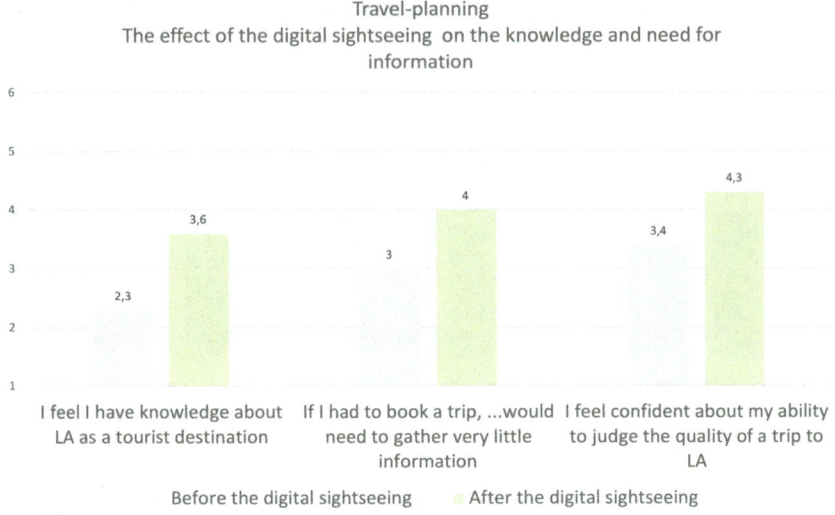

Fig. 5.4 The effect of the digital experience on the need for travel planning

tourist destination. The quality of the guest–host interaction is an important component for travellers. In a digital application, it is not easy to replicate this human component, the face-to-face interactions. We recognise this aspect, but it was not addressed in the travel survey presented in the next section.

DIGITAL TRAVEL APPLICATIONS—A SURVEY ON BEHAVIOURS AND ATTITUDES

The survey was targeted at a cross-section of citizens from Norway. We invited respondents from panels that recruit from the general population. The email invitation had the title "A travel survey – about visiting places digitally". As a consequence, we can assume that some that were invited, but with no or little interested in travel, overlooked the email invitation. Most employees have paid vacations of typically four weeks in the summer period. However, the restrictions caused by the pandemic have influenced and made vacation planning more difficult. In particular his is the case for international travel. This also means that what we refer to as digital travel might be an alternative for some. In total, 208 answered our survey. Two respondents were excluded due to incomplete answers. In this chapter we report on the answers of 206 respondents.

The survey had the following four sections; the profile of the respondents, travel plans, their view of digital tourist applications before, during or after a trip and also the role of a privately administered vaccine. Since international travel is only allow for fully vaccinated or travellers with a negative COVID-19 test, there has been a demand for taking a vaccine outside of the national health provision.

We present the survey findings for the age groups 16–29 years old, 30–49 years old, the 50–70 years old, and for all participants named "All". As for the population, the survey had 50% women and 50% men. For level of education, approximately 25% are in each of the groups—see figure A. As was expected, it was the 16–29 years old group who had the highest share of primary education only. In general, the educational profile, the age and gender distribution of the participants represent the national population quite well—see Figs. 5.5 and 5.6.

Digital meetings have become normal. There are many platforms for digital meetings and students and employees are often required to use a digital platform for meetings. As show in Fig. 5.7 approximately 80% have

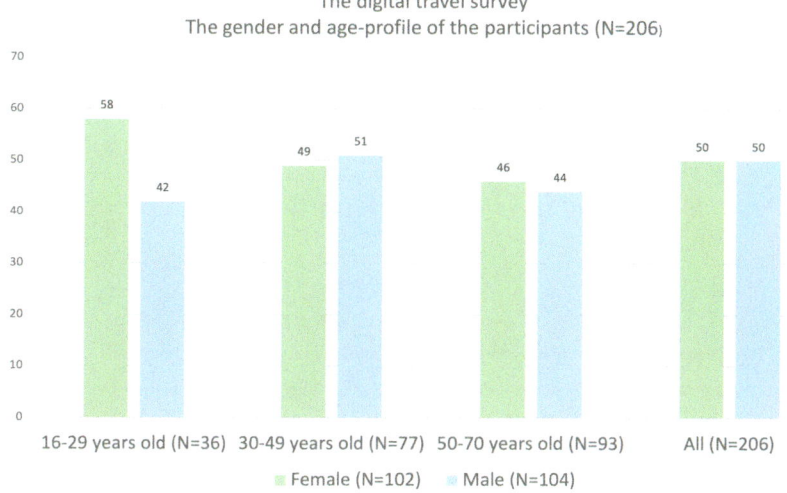

Fig. 5.5 The participants—age and gender

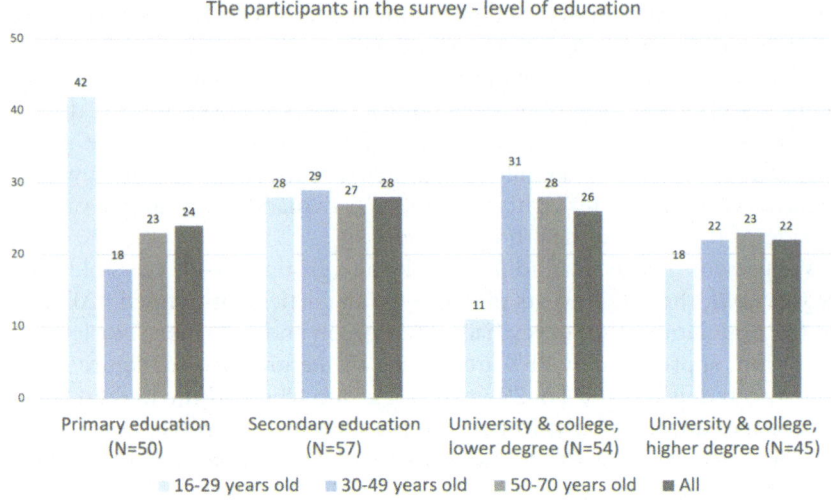

Fig. 5.6 The participants—age and education

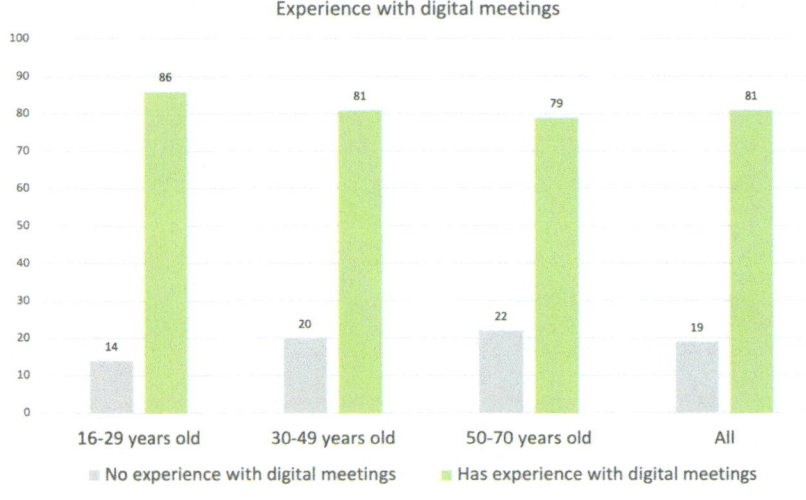

Fig. 5.7 Experience with digital meetings

had experience with digital meetings. It is a high number that reflects the fact that the pandemic has had a significant impact on the use of digital meetings.

Not all have the time and resources to have holidays many times a year, but for some travel has a high priority. Figure 5.8 shows that 2 or 3 times a year is quite common with 26 and 16% for all. For the youngest age group 42% answered once a year and only 3% three times or more.

Due to the pandemic, there has been a number of restrictions for travel in particular for international travel. At the time of the survey, July 2021, international travel was allowed, but due to a risk of being infected, many preferred to postpone the vacation. Instead, short distance travel and travel within the national boarders were much more common. This is reflected in the answers—approximately 50% had not planned a vacation, see Fig. 5.9.

Of all the participants only 10% had planned a vacation abroad—see Fig. 5.10. This is in accordance with findings in similar national surveys that report that 8–13% have planned a trip abroad.

In most cases fully vaccinated citizens can travel abroad and avoid quarantine even when the country visited has a high level of infections. However, the majority of citizens under the age of 45 had not been

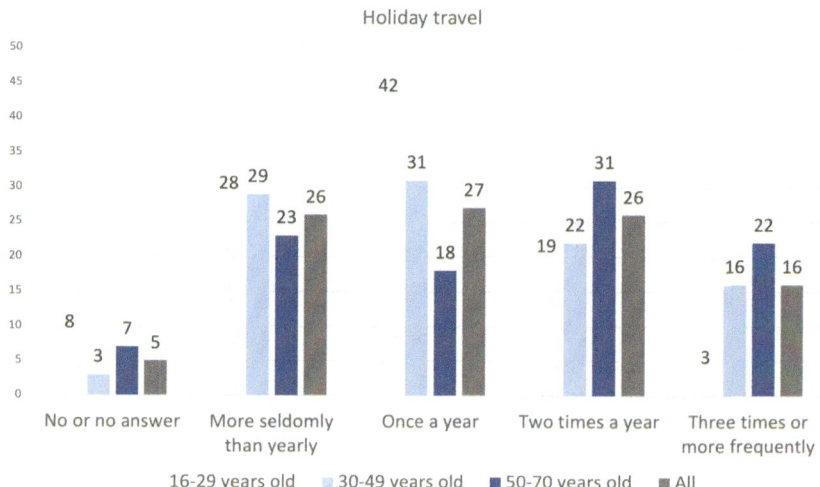

Fig. 5.8 Frequency of holiday travel per year

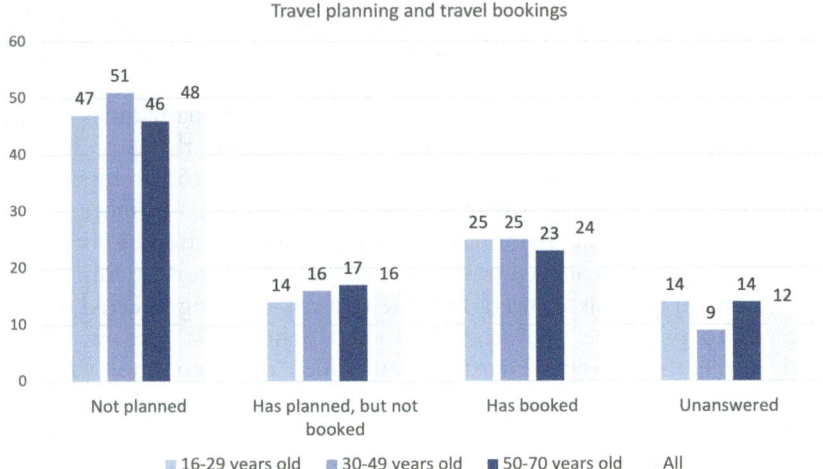

Fig. 5.9 Travel planning 2021

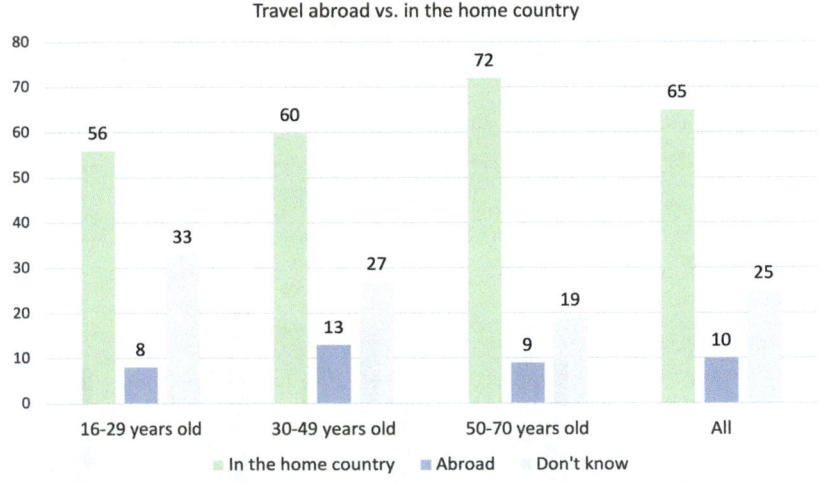

Fig. 5.10 Holiday destinations

offered two doses of the vaccine at the time of the survey. For the 16–29 years old, 44% were waiting for the first dose—see Fig. 5.11. This is the background for the question about willingness to take a vaccine privately to make travel easier.

Taken together, for the answers "maybe" and "yes, I would take a private vaccine", it is the 30–49 years olds that respond most positively to this alternative, 13%—see Fig. 5.12. The government and the health authorities have been warning the citizens against vaccines that are not offered by the health authorities. Still, for the age groups 30–49 years old, a total of 25% will take or will consider a private vaccine. This indicates that travel is important to them. It is not only recommendations by the government, restrictions and quarantines that matter. One of the reasons that motivate citizens to take a vaccine is travel.

For travel information, the Internet has for many years played a key role in planning, booking and communication about travel services. Digital travel apps and virtual tourism applications can be seen as information sources in travel context. Figure 5.13 illustrates whether the vacation planner uses information sources with geographical or place information.

For the question about information sources, we asked about Google street view or similar applications that have geographical information

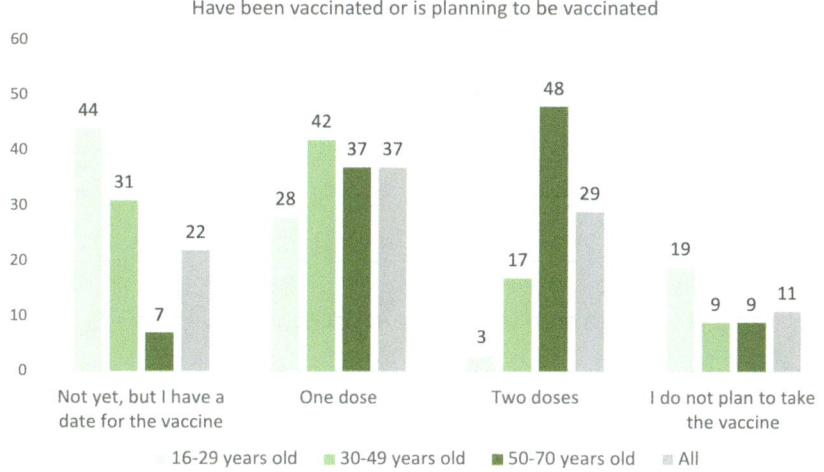

Fig. 5.11 The vaccination and age-groups

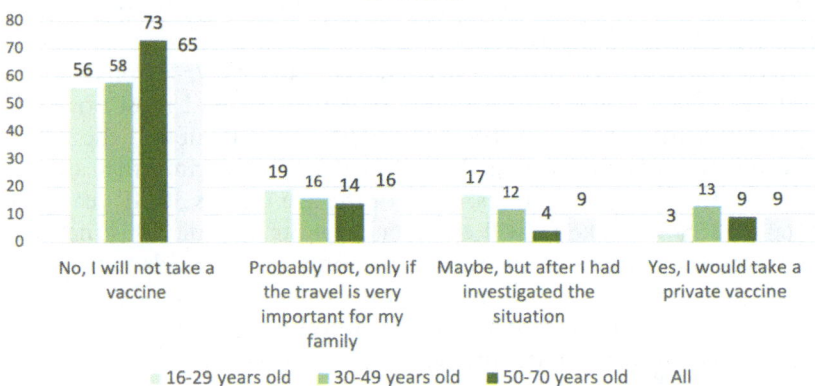

Fig. 5.12 Private vaccination and travel

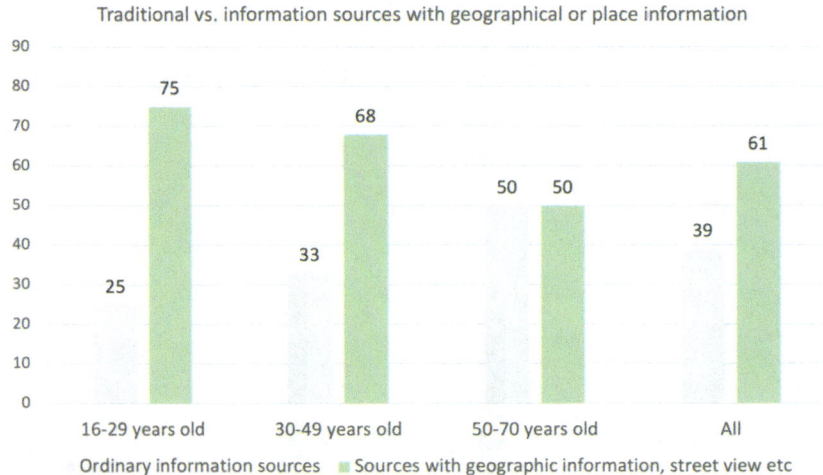

Fig. 5.13 Sources of geographical information and information that can create a sense of place

about where hotels, attractions and sights are. This kind of application can create a sense of place. As shown in Fig. 5.14, quite few have used virtual travel apps.

The core section of the survey contained questions about digital travel applications, virtual tourism and presentations or applications that can be regarded as travel products. We wrote an introduction to explain some of the terms, that the purpose of some of these travel applications can be to create a feeling of being there or to be a substitute for the travel. A digital meeting is not the same as meeting the person face-to-face, but the digital meeting can have many of the same characteristics. A vacation is also about getting away from where you live. Therefore, to visit a museum or attraction digitally is not a substitute for the vacation, but is an example of a digital travel.

We distinguished between the presentation, what it is like and, in the following question the experience itself. We asked about museums, hotels, attractions and guided tours, one at a time. The role of many travel and tourism companies is to the get people to travel, to get them to book trips and travel to the destination. Therefore, advertising and marketing are key factors for these businesses. We used the word "pre-taste" (of the experience) to indicate that it is more than just the presentation of

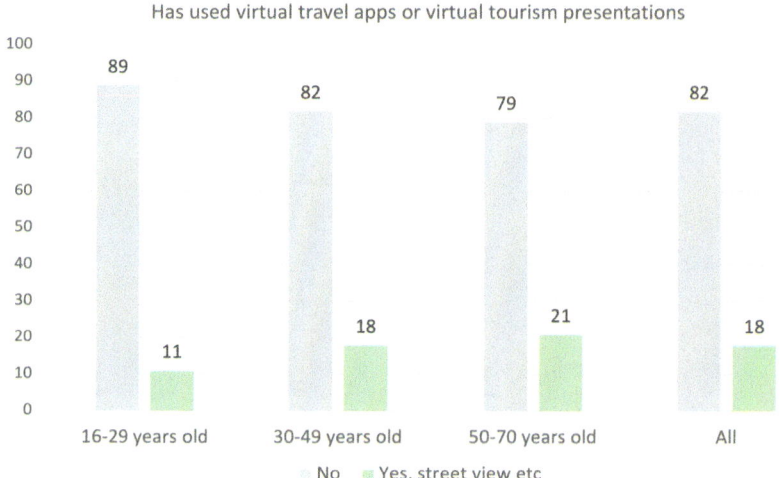

Fig. 5.14 The use travel apps or virtual presentations

information and plain facts—the presentation is intended to let the person feel what it is like to visit the place. A pre-taste is not a means to an end; the purpose is to create an interest and or to influence the person to book a trip. As a digital meeting can sometimes be a substitute for a meeting in person, a digital travel product can be a substitute for the experience in situ.

Most museums have online presentations with pictures or videos of their exhibitions. Some replicate the museum more accurately and create digital presentations intended to give the user a feeling of being in the museum. This is the backdrop of the first question about digital museums' presentations.

For the respondents view on digital presentations of a museum or an attraction, 58% of the 30–49 years old and 46% of the 50–70 years old choose "pre-taste of the experience". For the 16–29 years old, "marketing" was the most typical answer with 58% (see Fig. 5.15). Quite few, only 2%, answered that the experience can be a substitute for the in situ experience. But for the related question about subjective feeling of the experience compared to the in situ experience, 22% of the 30–49 years old, 17% of the 16–29 years old and 13% of the 50–70 years old answered that it can be similar to the in situ experience (Fig. 5.16).

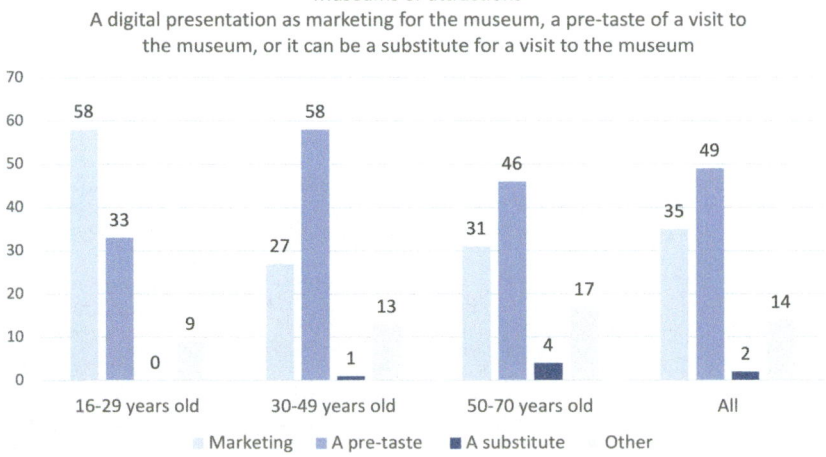

Fig. 5.15 Digital presentations of museums or other attractions

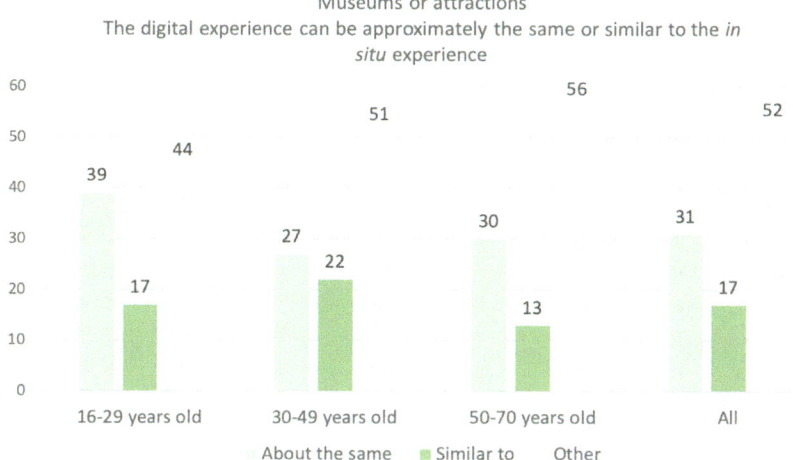

Fig. 5.16 Museums and other attractions—the digital experience in comparison to the in situ experience

For hotels, 48% of the 50–70 years old and 43% of the 30–49 years old answered "a pre-taste" while 58% of the 16–29 years old answered "marketing". An insignificant number, 1%, answered "a substitute" for a visit to a hotel—see Fig. 5.17. For obvious reasons the need for accommodation cannot be substituted digitally, but exploring what the hotel is like, the building, the location, etc., is relevant. Generally, a substantial part of the travel budget concerns accommodation and the 50 plus are normally more willing to pay for a good and central hotel compared to the younger generations. For activities, it was essentially the same pattern as for hotels (see Fig. 5.18).

For activities and the question whether or not the digital experience can be about the same or similar to the actual experience, 9% answered "similar to" and 21% "about the same"—see Fig. 5.19. The differences between the age groups were small.

It is quite common to take part in guided tours while visiting a destination. The next question was about a digital guided tour; is it similar to, a pre-taste, or a substitute for a physical guided tour.

For this question, there are differences between the age groups with the highest number for the 50–70 years old. For this age group 55% of answered "a pre-taste" for a digital version of a guided tour—see

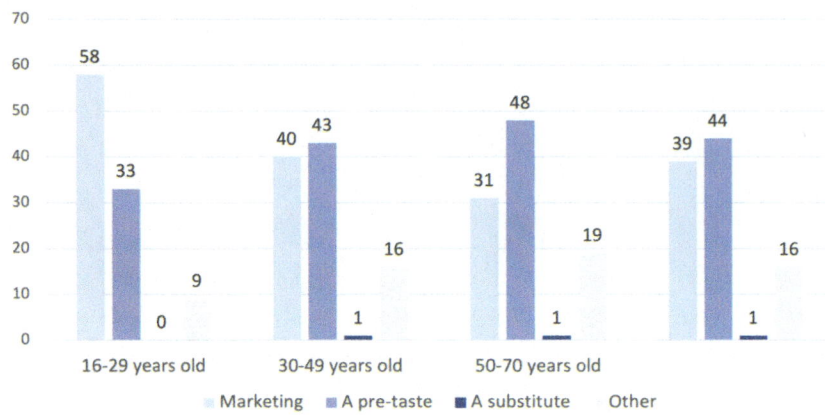

Fig. 5.17 Digital presentations of a hotel

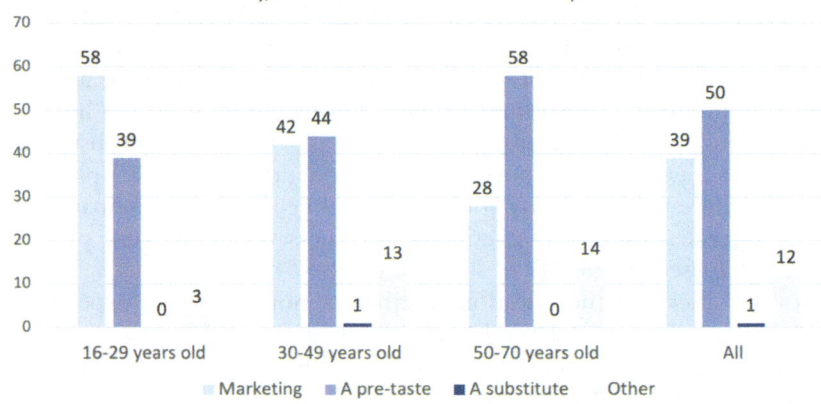

Fig. 5.18 Digital presentations of activities

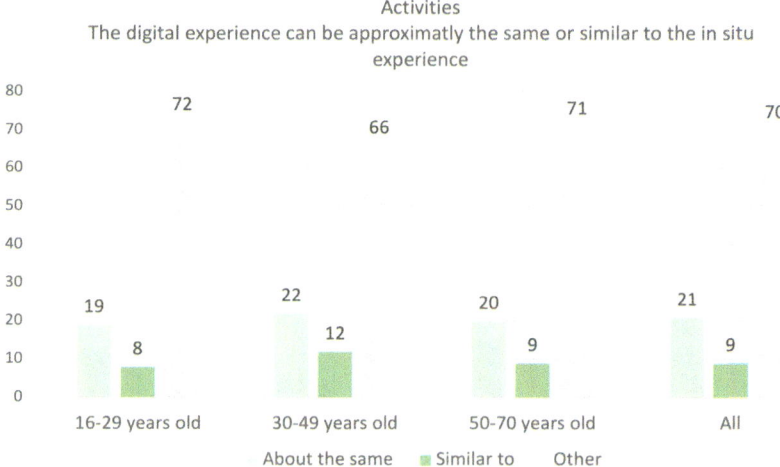

Fig. 5.19 Activities—the digital experience in comparison to the in situ experience

Fig. 5.20. For the 30–49 years old, 47% answered "a pre-taste" and for the 16–9 years old 42% answered in the same way.

For the question about whether or not the digital guided tour experience is about the same or similar to the in situ experience, 27% answered "about the same" and 18% "similar to" with only minor differences between the age groups (Fig. 5.21). Of the different types of destinations, the respondents gave the most positive answers for the digital alternatives for museums and guided tours. Most travellers take pictures or videos, with cameras or phones. Quite few, 8% thought that digital travel applications can be better than the traveller's own pictures and videos—see Fig. 5.22.

After the questions about experiences with and opinions about current digital travel applications, we asked about the role of digital travel applications in the future. The answers to these questions are not easy to interpret. To predict what will happen in the future in a longer time frame is guesswork, but it gives an indication of what kind of expectations for the future the respondents have.

The expectation is that digital travel applications will play a role in the planning phase—44% answered with this alternative, but with significant differences between the age groups, see Fig. 5.23. For "while travelling",

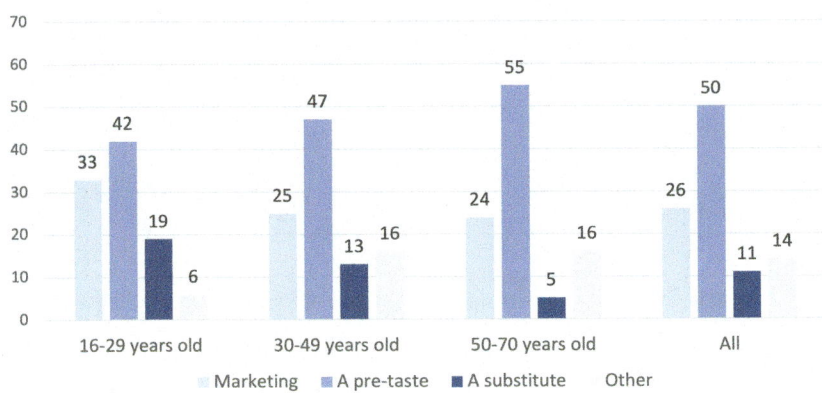

Fig. 5.20 Digital presentations of guided tours

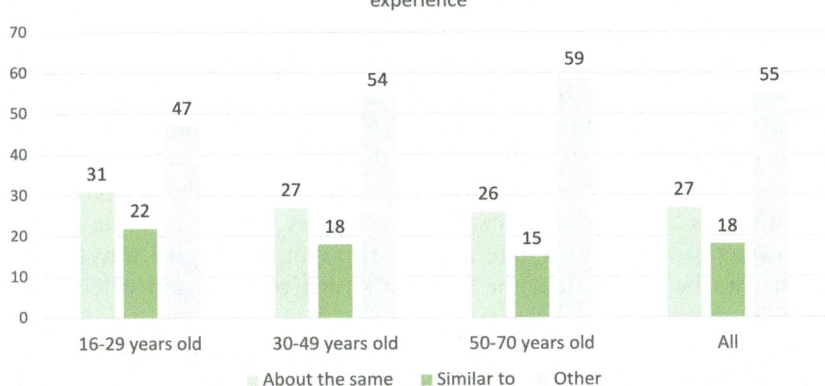

Fig. 5.21 Guided tours—the digital experience in comparison to the in situ experience

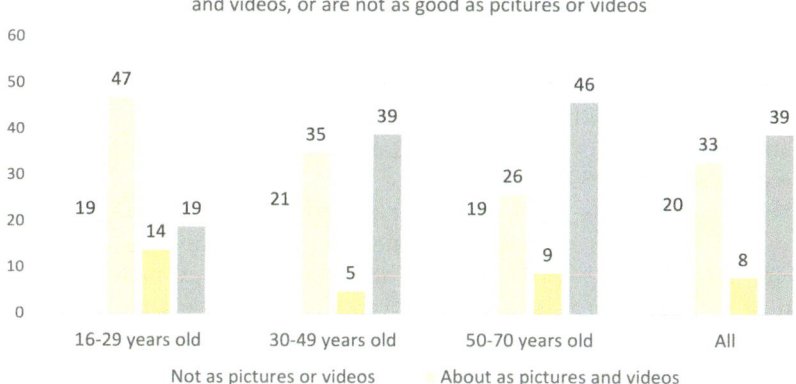

Fig. 5.22 Digital travel applications for sharing and re-experience the vacation

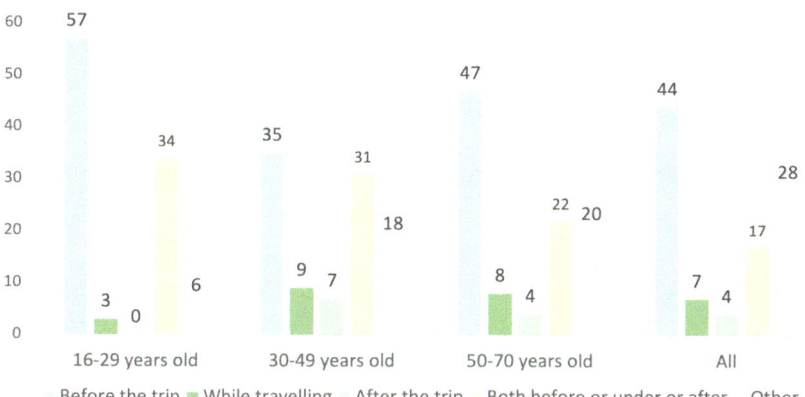

Fig. 5.23 Digital travel applications in the future—expectations

however, we find low numbers for all three age-groups.

Figure 5.24 shows that 40% indicate a willingness to pay for digital travel products for historical places, sights and to avoid queues.

Questions about willingness to pay are also hard to interpret. Some will not reveal what they actually are willing to pay because they believe that it is better to indicate a low price to avoid high prices. In total, 68% indicated that they are willing to pay 10% of the ticket prices at the destination—see Fig. 5.25.

The answers to the question about arguments for digital travel was coded by the authors. 67% did not mention any positive arguments—see Fig. 5.26. Some 14% wrote that there are good arguments without mention any. There are some positive arguments, such as that less travel is good for the environment, and there are barriers due to disabilities, illness and old age that favour digital travel.

But the majority is not convinced or very interested in a digital alternative to actual travel. Figures 5.27 and 5.28 show that there is a small segment, 10–20%, who believe that they, in the future, will use digital travel products that create an experience similar to the in situ experience. We can name this group "digital travellers".

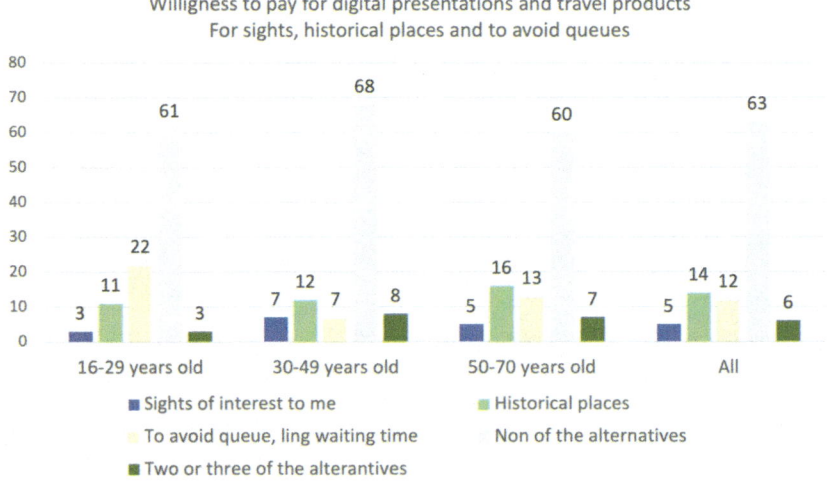

Fig. 5.24 Willingness to pay for digital travel pro

Fig. 5.25 Willingness to pay for digital travel products – a comparison to ticket prices of a service at the travel destination

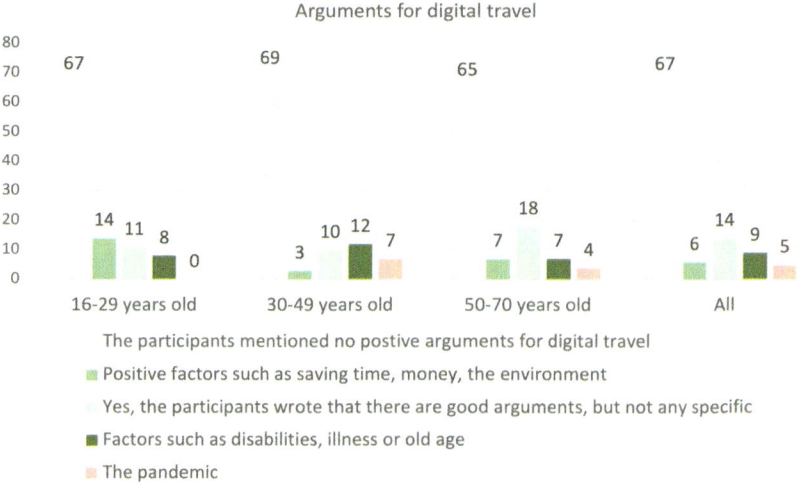

Fig. 5.26 Arguments for digital travel

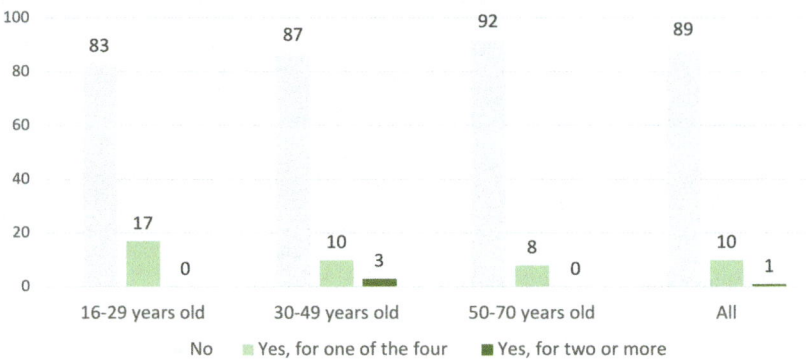

Fig. 5.27 Digital travel—a substitute for the in situ experience

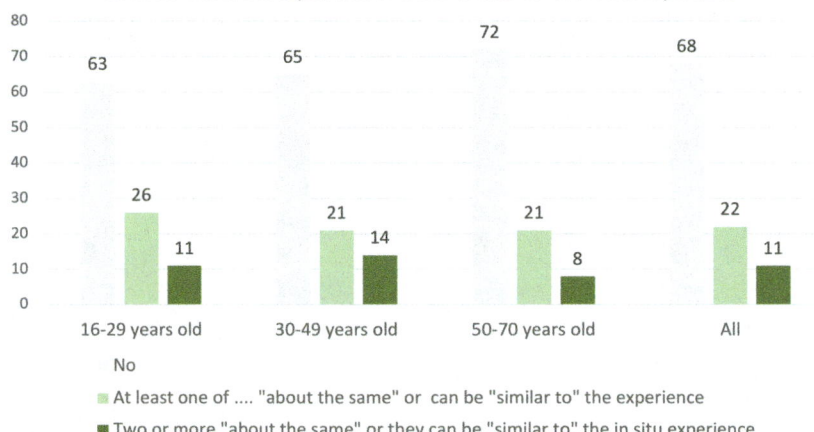

Fig. 5.28 The digital travel experience—similar to the in situ experience?

CONCLUSIONS

As to why we experience the feeling being there, in Chapter 2 we drew attention to theoretical contributions by James J. Gibson and Maurice Merleau-Ponty and many others who have discussed perception and the role of the senses. In the empirical studies we have used the Temple Presence Inventory, a measurement that includes perceptual realism about the five senses as one factor. We conclude that the perceptual mediated experience is actually similar to the unmediated experience. This is not always the case but, for those experiencing a high level of telepresence, all senses can be evoked—not only the visual and the audio senses that are directly stimulated by the technology.

Based on the findings from the empirical studies, and the Los Angeles study in particular, that not for all but for many of the subjects, the individuals that *"visited the city on the screen"*, the digital sightseeing, had the feeling of being there in the moment. The telepresence experience was evoked by the VE and it seems that the experience of place was perceived as real to the user in the intuitive phase when the digital sightseeing took place. We also found through our survey a group of people that we refer to as digital travellers.

Looking forward, with the possibilities of advanced technology in mind, what our survey reveals seems not unlikely. There are many ways in which digital travel can be developed further, just as there are a range of different ways in which the current situation of digital meetings can be improved. We cover this topic—of how to design digital travel and meetings so that they match the psychosocial needs of their participants—in Chapter 6.

REFERENCES

Adler, J. (1989). Origins of sightseeing. *Annals of Tourism Research, 16*(1), 7–29. https://doi.org/10.1016/0160-7383(89)90028-5

Bearden, W. O., Lichtenstein, D. R., & Teel, J. E. (1984). Comparison price, coupon, and brand effects on consumer reactions to retail newspaper advertisements. *Journal of Retailing, 60*(2), 11–34.

Benyon, D., Smyth, M., O'Neill, S., McCall, R., & Carroll, F. (2006). The place probe: Exploring a sense of place in real and virtual environments. *Presence: Teleoperators and Virtual Environments, 15*(6), 668–687. https://doi.org/10.1162/pres.15.6.668

Burke, R. R., Harlam, B. A., Kahn, B. E., & Lodish, L. M. (1992). Comparing dynamic consumer choice in real and computer-simulated environments. *Journal of Consumer Research, 19*(1), 71. https://doi.org/10.1086/209287

Clemenson, G. D., Wang, L., Mao, Z., Stark, S. M., & Stark, C. E. L. (2020). Exploring the spatial relationships between real and virtual experiences: What transfers and what doesn't. *Frontiers in Virtual Reality, 1,* 572122. https://doi.org/10.3389/frvir.2020.572122

Cohen, E. (1979). Rethinking the sociology of tourism. *Annals of Tourism Research, 6*(1), 18–35. https://doi.org/10.1016/0160-7383(79)90092-6

de Freitas, S., & Griffiths, M. (2008). The convergence of gaming practices with other media forms: What potential for learning? A review of the literature. *Learning, Media and Technology, 33*(1), 11–20. https://doi.org/10.1080/17439880701868796

Dormans, J. (2011). Beyond iconic simulation. *Simulation & Gaming, 42*(5), 610–631. https://doi.org/10.1177/1046878111426963

Dunn Ross, E. L., & Iso-Ahola, S. E. (1991). Sightseeing tourists' motivation and satisfaction. *Annals of Tourism Research, 18*(2), 226–237. https://doi.org/10.1016/0160-7383(91)90006-W

Gackenbach, J., & Bown, J. (2011). Video Game presence as a function of genre: A preliminary inquiry. *The Journal of the Canadian Game Studies Association, 5*(8), 4–28.

Gorini, A., Capideville, C. S., De Leo, G., Mantovani, F., & Riva, G. (2011). The role of immersion and narrative in mediated presence: The virtual hospital experience. *Cyberpsychology, Behavior, and Social Networking, 14*(3), 99–105. https://doi.org/10.1089/cyber.2010.0100

Howlett, S., Lee, R., & O'Sullivan, C. (2005). A framework for comparing task performance in real and virtual scenes. In *Proceedings of the 2nd symposium on applied perception in graphics and visualization—APGV '05,* 119. https://doi.org/10.1145/1080402.1080423

Jong, M. S. Y., Lee, J. H. M., & Shang, J. (2013). Educational use of computer games: Where we are, and what's next. In R. Huang, Kinshuk, & J. M. Spector (Eds.), *Reshaping learning* (pp. 299–320). Springer Berlin Heidelberg. https://doi.org/10.1007/978-3-642-32301-0_13

Khenak, N., Vezien, J., & Bourdot, P. (2020). Spatial presence, performance, and behavior between real, remote, and virtual immersive environments. *IEEE Transactions on Visualization and Computer Graphics, 26*(12), 3467–3478. https://doi.org/10.1109/TVCG.2020.3023574

Lombard, M., Ditton, T., & Crane, D. (2000). Measuring presence: A literature-based approach to the development of a standardized paper-and-pencil instrument. ... *on Presence, Delft,* .... http://www.socialinformation.org/readings/presence/measruingpresence.pdf

Lombard, M., Ditton, T. B., & Weinstein, L. (2009). Measuring presence: The temple presence inventory. In *Proceedings, twelfth international workshop on presence (ISPR 2009)*.

Lombard, M., Ditton, T. B., & Weinstein, L. (2011). Measuring telepresence: The validity of The Temple Presence Inventory (TPI) in a gaming context. In *Proceedings. Fourteenth international workshop on presence (ISPR 2011)*.

Lyu, S., & Farid, H. (2005). How realistic is photorealistic? *IEEE Transactions on Signal Processing, 53*(2), 845–850. https://doi.org/10.1109/TSP.2004.839896

Maejima, A., Yarimizu, H., Kubo, H., & Morishima, S. (2010). Automatic generation of head models and facial animations considering personal characteristics. In *Proceedings of the 17th ACM symposium on virtual reality software and technology—VRST '10*, 71. https://doi.org/10.1145/1889863.1889875

Mania, K., & Chalmers, A. (2001). The effects of levels of immersion on memory and presence in virtual environments: A reality centered approach. *CyberPsychology & Behavior, 4*(2), 247–264. https://doi.org/10.1089/109493101300117938

McKee, R. (2003). Storytelling that moves people: A conversation with screenwriting coach. *Harvard Business Review, 80*, 51–55.

Nisenfield, S. (2003). *Using reality to evaluate the ITC presence questionnaire* (Master thesis), Brown University. https://cs.brown.edu/research/pubs/theses/masters/2003/nisenfeld.pdf

Relph, E. (1976). *Place and placelessness*. SAGE.

Relph, E. (2007). Spirit of place and sense of place in virtual realities. *Techné: Research in Philosophy and Technology, 10*(3), 17–25. https://doi.org/10.5840/techne20071039

Schwartz, L. (2006). Fantasy, realism, and the other in recent video games. *Space and Culture, 9*(3), 313–325. https://doi.org/10.1177/1206331206289019

Seamon, D. (1982). The phenomenological contribution to environmental psychology. *Journal of Environmental Psychology, 2*(2), 119–140. https://doi.org/10.1016/S0272-4944(82)80044-3

Seamon, D. (1996). A singular impact: Edward Relph's place and placelessness. *Environmental and Architectural Phenomenology Newsletter, 7*(3), 5–8.

Seamon, D. (2000). A way of seeing people and place: Phenomenology in environment-behavior research. In S. Wapner, J. Demick, T. Yamamoto, & H. Minami (Eds.), *Theoretical perspectives in environment-behavior research* (pp. 157–178). Springer US. https://doi.org/10.1007/978-1-4615-4701-3_13

Seamon, D. (2018). Merleau-Ponty, lived body, and place: Toward a phenomenology of human situatedness. In T. Hünefeldt & A. Schlitte (Eds.), *Situatedness and place* (Vol. 95, pp. 41–66). Springer International Publishing. https://doi.org/10.1007/978-3-319-92937-8_4

Shamai, S. (1991). Sense of place: An empirical measurement. *Geoforum, 22*(3), 347–358. https://doi.org/10.1016/0016-7185(91)90017-K

Smith, D. C., & Park, C. W. (1992). The effects of brand extensions on market share and advertising efficiency. *Journal of Marketing Research, 29*(3), 296. https://doi.org/10.2307/3172741

Smith, M. K. (2006). Space, place and placelessness in the culturally regenerated city. In G. Richards (Eds.), *Cultural tourism*. Routledge.

Smyth, M., Benyon, D., McCall, R., O'Neill, S., & Carroll, F. (2015). Patterns of place: An integrated approach for the design and evaluation of real and virtual environments. In M. Lombard, F. Biocca, J. Freeman, W. IJsselsteijn, & R. J. Schaevitz (Eds.), *Immersed in media* (pp. 237–260). Springer International Publishing. https://doi.org/10.1007/978-3-319-10190-3_10

Sommerseth, H. (2007). Gamic realism: Player, perception and action in video game play. In *DiGRA '07—Proceedings of the 2007 DiGRA International Conference: Situated play* (Vol. 4, pp. 765–768). The University of Tokyo.

Suh, K.-S., & Chang, S. (2006). User interfaces and consumer perceptions of online stores: The role of telepresence. *Behaviour & Information Technology, 25*(2), 99–113. https://doi.org/10.1080/01449290500330398

Tian-Cole, S., & Cromption, J. (2003). A conceptualization of the relationships between service quality and visitor satisfaction, and their links to destination selection. *Leisure Studies, 22*(1), 65–80. https://doi.org/10.1080/02614360306572

Tjostheim, I. (2020). *Experiencing sense of place in a virtual environment: Real in the moment?* (Report RR-20.02). Umeå Universitet.

Tjostheim, I., & Haugland, B. (2005). *What do you plan to buy in the store today? Impulse buying in grocery stores: The challenge for market research*. Retailing Industry—Store wars, ESOMAR, Budapest.

Tjostheim, I., & Saether-Larsen, H. (2005). *How to validate a new MR tool? A case study in FMCG. Innovate*.

Turner, P., & Turner, S. (2006). Place, sense of place, and presence. *Presence: Teleoperators and Virtual Environments, 15*(2), 204–217. https://doi.org/10.1162/pres.2006.15.2.204

Turner, P., Turner, S., & Burrows, L. (2013). Creating a sense of place with a deliberately constrained virtual environment. *International Journal of Cognitive Performance Support, 1*(1), 54. https://doi.org/10.1504/IJCPS.2013.053554

Turner, P., Turner, S., & Carroll, F. (2005). The tourist gaze: Towards contextualised virtual environments. *Spaces, Spatiality and Technology* (pp. 281–297). KluwerSpringer.

Weick, K. E. (1995). *Sensemaking in organizations*. SAGE Publications.

Widyarto, S., & Latiff, S. A. M. (2007). The use of virtual tours for cognitive preparation of visitors: A case study for VHE. *Facilities, 25*(7/8), 271–285. https://doi.org/10.1108/02632770710753316

Woodside, A. G., Cruickshank, B. F., & Dehuang, N. (2007). Stories visitors tell about Italian cities as destination icons. *Tourism Management, 28*(1), 162–174. https://doi.org/10.1016/j.tourman.2005.10.026

Woodside, A. G., & Megehee, C. M. (2010). Advancing consumer behaviour theory in tourism via visual narrative art: Advancing consumer behaviour theory. *International Journal of Tourism Research, 12*(5), 418–431. https://doi.org/10.1002/jtr.762

Open Access This chapter is licensed under the terms of the Creative Commons Attribution 4.0 International License (http://creativecommons.org/licenses/by/4.0/), which permits use, sharing, adaptation, distribution and reproduction in any medium or format, as long as you give appropriate credit to the original author(s) and the source, provide a link to the Creative Commons license and indicate if changes were made.

The images or other third party material in this chapter are included in the chapter's Creative Commons license, unless indicated otherwise in a credit line to the material. If material is not included in the chapter's Creative Commons license and your intended use is not permitted by statutory regulation or exceeds the permitted use, you will need to obtain permission directly from the copyright holder.

CHAPTER 6

When the Virtual Becomes Real?

Abstract In the first part of this final chapter, we look at several current trends in technologies used to enable various forms of digital travel, and some recent innovations—including social telepresence robots, drones, holograms and immersive VR. We briefly describe the approach and evaluate the pros and cons and potential of each, then move on to speculations about future directions and new possibilities. We present a method of stimulating new design ideas for digital travel, based on metaphors and blending theory. We illustrate the method using the metaphor: "*To use my device is to travel*". In the second part of the chapter, we recap and finalise our journey through the book.

Keywords Social telepresence robots · Drones · Holograms · Immersive VR · Metaphor · Blends

INTRODUCTION

The restrictions on meetings and travel that have come with the COVID-19 pandemic have led to enormous change in behaviour and attitudes about the practicality and acceptability of replacing physical encounters with virtual ones. Many different kinds of meetings take place without physical travel; for example, concerts, school and college classes, sports events, academic and other conferences, training and personal development courses. What do we mean by "take place"? As introduced in Chapter 1, Meyrowitz (1986) described how modern communication media commonly lack a sense of place for the communicants. He suggested that they do not really have face-to-face meetings, since the participants are in different physical places and do not share an experience of being in the same place. The meetings do not "take place". They also lack the elements of departure, passage and arrival that characterise travel (Leed, 1991). In this section, we outline the strengths and weaknesses of using digital technology to meet others without having the sensation of travel.

Having meetings without physically being in the same place as the other participants saves time and resources; it is also relatively good for the environment. However, it is no accident that "Zoom fatigue" has become a common term for the exhaustion many people feel after spending much time in digitally mediated meetings (whether on Zoom or some other technological platform). One reason might be that, since people travel less currently, they spend more time in meetings overall. But there are several other possible reasons that reflect the psychosocial reality of digital meetings.

Bailenson (2021) identified four main reasons for what he calls "nonverbal overload". Firstly, with the typical laptop or desktop computer configuration used for such meetings, people experience too much, very close, eye contact, often with people we don't know well. Secondly, seeing oneself during social interactions is unnatural, and results in self-consciousness and self-dissatisfaction, which is also fatiguing. Thirdly, we move less, and bodily movements normally aid our cognition and sense of comfort. Finally, because of the absence of natural nonverbal cues, for example, related to eye-contact and head movements, video meetings are more cognitively demanding and therefore tiring. A recent study by Fauville et al. (2021) found that women generally suffer more Zoom fatigue than men, partly because they tend to have longer meetings and shorter breaks, and also because they are more sensitive to seeing their own video image in this social context.

Face-to-face digital meetings are not really face-to-face, because, as Meyrowitz (1986) pointed out, the participants are not physically together. Only the face is seen, the rest of the body is out of view, whereas in physical meetings our whole bodies participate to provide nonverbal cues that help people communicate.

Another issue with digital interaction with distant others is lag—a delay introduced by the communication network. Even though the time lag between exchanges is generally less than was the case with old telephonic systems, it still affects interaction. It is well known (e.g. Short et al., 1976) that a perceptible delay in a person's responses can give the impression of hesitancy, perhaps even dishonestly (since we tend to delay when reflecting before responding, and this might be the time needed to come up with a less than honest answer). There is a measurable negative effect on social presence (Cui, et al., 2013). The typical lag on a modern teleconferencing system is around 0.6s, whereas to be imperceptible the lag needs to be less than 0.2s (Gunawardena, 1995). Lack of synchronisation between audio and video is also often a problem, with video "freezes" not being uncommon. Time and synchronisation issues add to the increase cognitive load of digital meetings, along with low fidelity or distorted sound and vision. This combination might also be expected to result in reduced memorability for digital communication, analogous to the effect found with synthetic speech (Waterworth & Thomas, 1985) since the increased cognitive load of accurately perceiving content reduces that available for mental interpretation and storage.

We can see several clear developments in the way people travel and meet, using digital technology. There are obvious and widespread developments, such as the expanded use of teleconferencing systems described above, accessed by computer, tablet and phone. These have been very successful in allowing a wide range of social activities to continue despite restrictions on travel. But, as outlined earlier in the book, they do not fully satisfy the psychosocial needs of their users. They are tiring and stressful for many. They do not provide a positive travel experience, a sense of being there, in another place with other people, away from the physical location of the body. We need to have the sense that we are embodied in another place, even though we are not. A variety of responses to this need have emerged already, which we outline in the rest of this section.

Recent Innovations in Digital Travel

In this section, we briefly outline two recent strands in ways of innovating digital travel. The first is represented by social telepresence robots and drones, the second by immersive VR and the use of holographic representations.

Social Telepresence Robots and Drones

The idea behind social telepresence robots is to combine functionalities common to teleconferencing systems with physical presence in a distant location via a robot. Their use in this way represents a set of approaches that stress the need for a proxy physical presence in the distant location, but downplay the need for a strong sense of psychological presence there. They have their roots in remote manipulation systems that provide both views of, and the capacity for surrogate action in, a remote location.

Tsui et al. (2011) describe social telepresence robots as "embodied video conferencing on wheels". The typical set up is for there to be a simple robot that can be controlled by a person in another location. The robot includes a video camera and a screen, on which the remote person's image (captured by the camera of their communication device) is displayed. Such an arrangement is typically used so that a person at home can "attend" a meeting in their place of employment, visit a public place such as a museum or conduct remote inspections at factories or hospitals. The remote person can move around the place (via the robot), observe people and things from different viewpoints, visit and speak to different people—for example, people in different offices or hospital beds—and be seen and heard by the people there, via the physical presence provided by the social telepresence robot.

Social telepresence robotics is an expanding field, although not many evaluative studies have been conducted as yet. In a few cases social robots have sometimes been given a human, or other animate-creature, form (Kristoffersson, 2013).

A recent qualitative study of the use of telepresence robots to relieve social isolation in older adults before and during the Covid-19 pandemic (Isabet et al., 2021) found that acceptance levels were good, although they drew no conclusions about whether the robots were more beneficial during the pandemic than before. They do, however, point to a number of issues that need to be investigated further, including usability and functionality for social interaction.

Social drones are in some ways a more flexible approach than the use of robots, since they can in principle go anywhere at any time—whereas there has be a robot positioned at a remote site for social interaction to be achieved. Shakeri and Neustaedter (2019) reported on a prototype system called Teledrone, which combines a drone and controlling interface with what is essentially a teleconferencing system. The envisaged use case was for distant participant to share in an outdoor activity, such as hiking, and drones clearly have the advantage of being able to cross and communicate over difficult terrain and bodies of water. According to the authors, "Teledrone provides an embodiment for a remote user and can help support spatial awareness" (from the abstract). In principle, this kind of approach can be used almost anywhere, even with the drone moving indoors or into confined spaces, although there may be safety issues when drones are used in this way.

Immersive VR Approaches and the Use of Holograms

At the time of writing, Oculus (the VR-technology company owned by Facebook) is using the slogan: "Defy reality and distance", which could stand as a general call to take up digital travel. Facebook CEO Mark Zuckerberg indicated in an article in The Verge (23 July, 2021) that he sees the future of Facebook as a "metaverse" company. According to the article, Zuckerberg said: "A lot of the meetings that we have today, you're looking at a grid of faces on a screen. That's not how we process things either". Describing how interacting in immersive virtual reality would change that situation, he is reported as saying: "You feel present with other people as if you were in other places, having different experiences that you couldn't necessarily do on a 2D app or webpage…".

Full-body immersion has some advantages, in that it is possible to convey a very rich sense of being in another place, but action in the remote place is problematic unless the place exists only virtually. It all has profound social disadvantages. Despite its power for conveying a sense of being in another place, there are inherent difficulties in using immersive VR from a variety of locations, especially public or social locations encountered physically in everyday life.

The more one is immersed in a virtual world, the more one is cut off from the physical world in which the body is located. Just wearing a head-mounted display can open up a distant place as if one were there—at least visually and auditorily. But it also renders the wearer vulnerable to any threats, dangers and social antagonism such as ridicule in the actual place the physical body is located. Where people are happy to escape from a dull situation into their phones—waiting for a bus or riding on an underground train—the same is unlikely to apply when wearing a head-mounted display. The power and attraction of phones and other mobile devices is partly that people can devote some attention to both the current physical world and the virtual happenings displayed on the device. The way these two worlds are mixed is far from optimal, both for the user or the other people involved (both locally and at a distance), but people manage, for example, to chat with distant others while finding their way through a train station. This would clearly not be the case with immersive VR.

Nevertheless, immersive VR of one kind or another is likely to become increasingly popular as an effective way of experiencing a distant place and events presented there, from a fixed and secure physical location; in the privacy of a home office, for example. In a completely virtual world, with full-body tracking and immersive displays, all kinds of action are possible, including some not possible with the body in the physical world, such as flying or passing through walls. Body tracking and immersive displays can also be combined with technologies such as robots or drones, allowing digital travel to actual places, though this needs to be carefully regulated because of obvious safety concerns.

The use of holograms is predicted to be the next big innovation in teleconferencing. In this set up, two or more locations are linked, as in a conventional teleconference, but participants in different locations see each other as holographic representations with a life-size 3D representation displayed in a specially equipped booth, rather than on a small screen (see e.g. Wired, 2021). The technology has been available for a decade or more, but is expected to become both more affordable and in great demand, largely due to changes in needs and attitudes brought about by restrictions in physical travel. While holograms might well become a fairly popular way of improving the vividness and intimacy of digital meetings, they are restricted to special, generally small, and expensively equipped rooms (or large booths) at both ends. Clearly, this is not compatible with flexible digital travel, either in terms of where one can be while travelling, or where one can travel to.

In contrast to the use of social telepresence robots and drones, immersive VR and holographic approaches both stress a vivid sense of psychological presence, but do not afford action in another physical place. They currently share a dependency on a fixed geographical location when interacting with distant people and places. This might change with the rapid pace of technological development, but social acceptance and safety concerns limit such use.

Rethinking Digital Travel

To conclude this section, we consider below the ways in which the physical and the virtual can be blended to support embodied interaction in integrated places that span distance boundaries, drawing on our theoretical account of the ways in which virtual experiences can be accepted as real by interactive participants. If experiences in such places can become real for the participants, virtual travel could in the future replace our current disjointed social interactions over the Internet.

We have suggested that immersive VR and other technologies are likely to become increasingly popular as reasonably effective ways of experiencing a distant place and events presented there. VR can provide the most vivid sense of presence in another place, but can only realistically be used from a fixed, secure private and physical location. Meeting and visiting at a distance, via mobile devices and laptops, are increasingly popular, but the experience is less convincing and satisfying as digital travel. In what ways can we combine digital possibilities with social and physical realities to overcome some of these shortcomings?

In the rest of this section we consider how we could experience people and places through digital technology in the future, in light of discussions and findings from earlier chapters as well as the trends identified above.

Metaphors and the Blending of Physical-Digital Realities

Travel implies a journey, which involves a departure, a passage and an arrival. In touristic trips, and other types of temporary visit, there is travel from home to another, distant place, and then a return home again. Before travel, there is preparation and anticipation; after travel, recollection and sharing. When applied to digital travel, this is the "home-away-back-home" metaphor (introduced in Chapter 1). The metaphor provides a starting point for designing more satisfactory ways of implementing digital travel. The most obvious of these is perhaps to mimic equivalent non-digital settings and interactions as closely as possible with appropriate technological capabilities and design, but this is both too ambitious and too limiting. It is too ambitious because far from everything about physical travel can be adequately simulated. It is too limiting because digital devices can transcend the restrictions of the physical (for example, with instant travel and instantaneous searches).

However digital travel is realised, technically, it can be seen as a blend of the digital and the physical. With immersive VR, the blend is almost entirely digital, but some physical elements remain, since the traveller moves her body in physical space while experiencing the consequences within a virtual world. At the other extreme, the blend represented by standard video conference systems, used on phones or laptops, is heavily weighted towards the physical—the place where the traveller is actually located. Digital travel blends also occupy a position on what can be called the action dimension—the extent to which the traveller can act in the world they visit. With a social telepresence robot, for example, the traveller can move around in physical space, talk to people and sometimes make gestures, whereas a visit to a theatrical performance may be very vivid, but with no possibilities for action in the witnessed performance.

Waterworth and Hoshi (2016) suggest an approach to the design of interactive presence in what they call "everyday blended reality". Applying this approach to designing new ways of realising digital travel would represent an explicit attempt to blend the reality of physical travel with that of the interactive possibilities of digital media and devices. There is no single direction in which digital travel can be expected to evolve, but we can begin to re-imagine future digital travel possibilities as a set of different blends of the physical world and selected functionalities of digital devices. In the rest of this subsection we consider how the design process might work, and speculate on the possible outcomes.

As described by Imaz and Benyon (2006) "designing with blends" starts with a metaphor. A common example from HCI research is the computer desktop metaphor. The user interface appearance, and to some extent the behaviour from a user's perspective, is presented as a desktop, with folders, a trash can, objects that can be moved or opened by the user and so on. This is the familiar WIMP (Windows, Icons, Menus and a Pointer) interface common to most PCs. It is said to be a result of applying the desktop metaphor to the user interface of an operating system. As in any metaphor, it is somewhat like the thing it conveys (a physical desktop), but also very different. Imaz and Benyon (2006) point out that, although this started as being seen as metaphorical, it is no longer. Rather a "desktop" or "laptop" has become a thing in itself; as they put it, following Fauconnier and Turner (1998), a new "emergent space"—a concept in its own right.

Designing with blends works as shown in Fig. 6.1. There is a generic (conceptual) space that reflects the abstract structure and organisation of

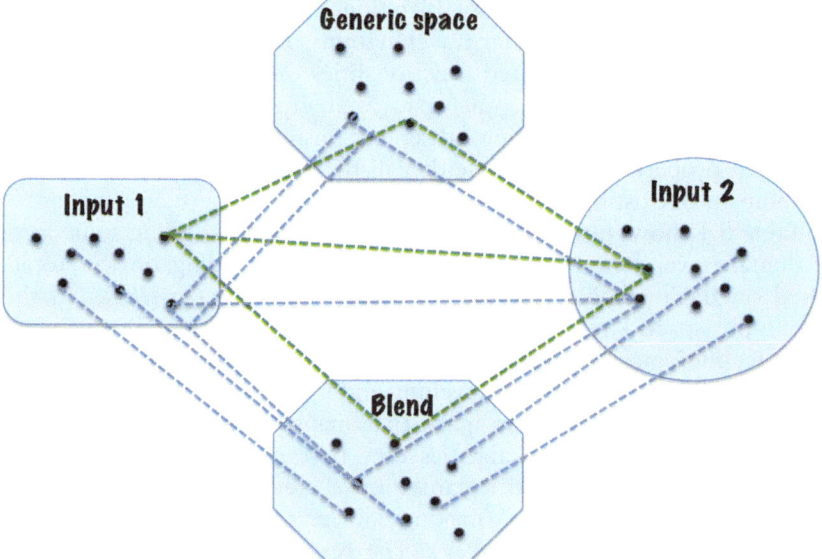

Fig. 6.1 Designing with blends

an overarching concept, such as in the above "desktop" example, office work. There are at least two "input" conceptual spaces, which in the same case might be "computer operations" and "physical office desktop". Each of these input spaces inherits some of the characteristics of the generic space, and also has other characteristics. A few of the characteristics are shared between the two input spaces; there is "cross-space mapping"; for example, "storage" and "trashing". Finally, some of the characteristics of the input spaces are merged into the blend, a new emergent structure; in this case this would be a high-level design space for an interface partially based on the metaphorical idea that a computer is a desktop; the familiar desktop we all use, and which is now not metaphorical, but a thing in itself. It is also possible to use two or more emergent blend spaces as inputs to further blending.

Waterworth and Hoshi (2016) used this approach to design "blended everyday realities" in which elderly users could interact, with technologies embedded in their environment, via ambient input objects and display devices, using simple movements and peripheral perception. In the same way, we can imagine the use of blending to create one or more top-level designs for future digital travel systems, combining some features of physical travel with selected functionalities of digital communications technologies. Blended conceptual space is an emergent conceptual structure that can incorporate new ideas and insights. It can include new emergent properties that exist neither in the world of physical travel nor the domain of existing interactive functionalities.

Table 6.1 shows how blending might work when designing some form of digital travel (one of many possible ways of blending on this topic) based on the metaphor *"To use my device is to be a traveller"*. In this case, input space-1 refers to the frame of ways of utilising current interactive technologies (functionalities of devices), input space-2 refers to the frame of conventional ways of travelling and input space-3 refers to aspects of embodiment. The generic space that maps onto each of the inputs contains some of the characteristics they have in common, and reflects more abstract structure and organisation shared by the inputs, that of navigating in physical space (making journeys, traversing distance and social interaction to find the way). The resultant blended space—HCI is travel (*To use my device is to be a traveller*)—is the start of a potentially new way of thinking about digital travel. There are many possible ways of deriving a blended space, depending on the metaphor chosen and

Table 6.1 Blending applied to the metaphor "To use my device is to be a traveller"

Generic space: Navigation	Input space 1: Tech features	Input space 2: Travel	Input space 3: Embodiment	Blended space: HCI is travel
Space	Sensors	Getting lost	Moving	3D Space
Topography	Messages	Distance	Gazing	Places
Landmarks	Input–output	Landmarks	Touching	Landmarks
Distance	Icons	Meetings	Hiding	Selection
Signposts	Selection	Time	Pointing	Moving
Meetings	Sound	Preparation	Turning	Leaving–arriving
Time	3D space	Leaving–arriving	Resting	Meeting
Danger	Animation	Sightseeing	Listening	Sightseeing
Movement	Gestures	Taking photos	Falling	Saving images
Leaving-arriving	Meetings	Remembering	Balancing	Sounds
Getting lost	Movement	Places	Placing	Input–output
Memory	Memory	Memory	Memory	Memory

the features selected from the two input spaces; there are thus very many possible new designs. It is also possible to blend the blends, by using the features of two (or more) blended spaces as the input spaces for further blending.

Several other metaphors seem promising as a basis for designing future blends. The following is an initial list of candidates:

- When I turn on my computer I become a traveller
- A videoconference is a short visit to another place
- Browsing the Internet is a journey
- My phone is my home
- My PC is a vehicle
- Interaction is an adventure
- I leave home when I use my device, then later I return
- When I visit digital places, I am inside and outside at the same time.

In the next section, we complete our journey through the book, concluding our argument that the feeling one is actually in a place—the feeling of "being there"—is vital to the quality and success of virtual social interactions and travels to distant (or fictional) places. This is especially relevant at times when travel is restricted or prohibited, since a lack of travel can mean few social opportunities, leading to a sense of isolation and sometimes depression. Currently, however, virtual travel is unlike physical travel in many significant respects, and does not adequately satisfy the socio-psychological needs of people meeting, of tourists and of other travellers. As we suggested above, new ways of thinking about digital travel are called for.

REFLECTING ON OUR JOURNEY SO FAR, AND OUR PLANS

Digital travel is about the sense of *being there*; being there without having to go there. We motivated our journey into this territory by noting that people increasingly travel, visit and meet other people in computer-mediated environments, and that this trend has been boosted by the covid-19 pandemic from 2020 onwards. Before that, videoconferencing and other technologies were already in widespread use by businesses and as a way for families and friends to keep in touch over distances. Recent developments have led to many other kinds of meetings and events taking place without physical travel. This trend seems likely to continue, with more and more people meeting and visiting places via digital environments and interactions. But, as we have suggested, current technologies for realising these kinds of digital travel do not succeed in matching the psychosocial needs of participants (Bailenson, 2021). In trying to understand and move on from this situation, we planned an itinerary for our journey via a series of waypoints; each of these allowing one facet of digital travel—*being there in a distant place*—to be examined in detail. We reflect on our journey through the book in the rest of this section.

Our first waypoint on our journey through the book was characterised by a focus on the *being* in being there. How can we be anywhere? It turns out that we cannot be without being somewhere, and that this is naturally the place in which our bodies are located. We presented different philosophical and psychological perspectives on having the experience of being somewhere, stressing the role of perception. The motivation for this was to shed light on ways of understanding the experience of being in another world created or mediated by digital technology. We looked at representationalism, relationism, enactivism and the sense-data view, and concluded that relationism offers the best understanding of perceptual illusions from an ordinary person's perspective, a popular way of defining telepresence experiences. We also suggested that enactivism is also very relevant to understanding presence, because it stresses that experiences are inseparable from the perceiver's bodily activities. Enactivism was heavily influenced by the work of Merleau-Ponty (1962). Both of these approaches have something to add to our understanding of the phenomena of digital travel. Representationalism is probably not well known to many readers, but it has a straightforward answer to many of the hard questions by claiming that what we see or experience are representations in the brain.

Moving on to more practical psychological perspectives, we introduced dual process theories of cognition (Kahneman, 2002; Stanovich & West, 2000), and suggested that acceptance of the reality of an external world, in the moment, is largely a result of intuitive, rapid cognitive processing. One for the first to observe this was the philosopher Baruch Spinoza.

Merleau-Ponty's views on perception (Merleau-Ponty, 1962), based in the relationship between the world, embodiment, action and perception, also led us into a focus on transparency in interactions with the world—technology that disappears from attention—and so with digitally mediated environments. Direct perception accounts of presence are appealing in the way embodiment is seen as linking mind and body, with perception understood as happening "out there", not in the brain, both in our perceptions of the physical world and of compellingly rendered virtual worlds. This a key idea for understanding how digital travel can be experienced as perceptually real. Enactivism and the direct perception approach both stress that the possibilities for action in the world are important for the experience of it. This, in turn, is influenced by the characteristics of the world in which we act, through what are known as affordances.

This brings us to our second waypoint, a consideration of the question: what is telepresence? How can technology provide us with the means to escape our bodies, in some sense, and be *there*—where "there" is another place, a place other than where our bodies are physically located? To address this question we compared and contrasted different theoretical accounts of telepresence, including presence as a pretence (a simulation of reality [Slater, 2009]), as pretending (making believe the virtual world is real [Turner 2016, Turner et al., 2016]), as a perceptual illusion ("the illusion of non-mediation" [Lombard & Ditton, 1997; Riva, 1999]), and as embodied attention to the surrounding (or apparently surrounding) environment. Waterworth et al. (2015, 2020) define presence as "the feeling of being located in a perceptible external world around the self", and suggest that "Varying feelings of presence reflect the extent to which attention is focused on the external environment". These views are all well-accepted in the field, and all can be seen as contributing to a virtual travel experience.

When we feel highly present, we believe in the perceived world in which we experience ourselves to be. In that moment it is real to us. Creating that effect is a key part of a convincing digital travel experience. To have that experience, we must be attending to the digital world, feeling as if we are (as-if-physically) surrounded by it. When that is achieved, our imaginations are involved in at least two ways: in how we perceive our surroundings, and in how we conceptualise our being there. While we do not think that we need to make-believe (that the world is real), we do use our imagination, and memory, to make sense of what happens there. The world may be a simulation, be veridical, be misperceived or even be an hallucination. In the moment of a vivid digital travel experience we do not reflect on this question, we just have the experience. But we do believe that it is veridical. When we later recall and talk about our experience, it is as if it were real. At the same time, we refer to it as a digital experience because we can reflect and reason that to have been the case.

Our next area of focus was characterised by an examination of notions of place, as outlined in work in tourism studies and other applied social fields, focusing on the factors affecting sense of place (Relph, 1976) and on how and when different experiences of place arise in the traveller. The aim was to understand the factors that can be expected to contribute to the digital experience of a distant place. Marketing and hedonic consumption were also seen to be useful in understanding travel and travellers (e.g. Hirschman & Holbrook, 1982; Holbrook & Hirschman, 1982), for example, through the mechanisms of expressed intentions to visit a place and word of mouth recommendations.

The tourist experience is an amalgam of different experiences (see, e.g., Cohen, 1979). It involves all senses and therefore their impact should not be overlooked in efforts to theorise tourism's experiential dimensions. A key question concerns the ways in which digital experiences are similar to or different from in situ experiences. We found that virtual travel is unlike physical travel in many significant respects, but the experience of a place—assuming the telepresence feeling of *being there* has been achieved, is psychosocially similar. For digital travel and digital experiences too, place attachment is a relevant concept for places that a person knows well. Put another way, a digital experience can become a spatial experience if our bodily senses are invoked by the virtual place. A key element in a memorable experience is perceived realness. We concluded that facts and accuracy have a similar role in digital experiences as in in situ experiences.

Our next stop was to consider empirical findings about the extent to which some current technologies can elicit a sense of presence, and place. We investigated and reported on factors affecting the sense of place experience, and telepresence, using a video game environment to facilitate sightseeing behaviour among participants in the study. We went on to explore in detail people's attitudes to physical travel and digital travel, both in the present and in the future. Interestingly, we were able to identify a subset of people whom we can already categorise as "digital travellers". What will they encounter on their future digital travels?

Finally, in the present chapter, we considered selected trends in technologies used to enable various forms of digital travel, before outlining an approach to thinking about new possibilities for implementing digital travel based on metaphors and blending theory.

Despite our view that digital travel opens up many new possibilities, we recognise that these may not be entirely benign. Nor do they always go one way, with the physical influencing the virtual experience. Some people are overwhelmed by awe when they visit a place they have read about in a novel, or seen in paintings. This may also happen with places that have been experienced in virtual reality, say when planning a trip. The actual place may overwhelm the visitor. On the other hand, the opposite effect is perhaps more usual; the carefully selected and presented glimpses of places experienced in digital promotional media may lead to the visitor being disappointed and less able to enjoy the real possibilities of the actual place. There may also be a kind of inverse presence (Timmins & Lombard, 2005), in which the actual place does not seem as real as a digital version. It may become the case for some that actual places do not seem real unless they can also be visited digitally. Physical places without Internet access (there are still many of these) may seem less real than other places, because visitors cannot share their experience of the place with distant others.

The more we are sharing our experiences of the moment with distant others, the less we may seem to be really there, where we physically are. This is one of the comforting aspects of ubiquitous use of a mobile phone: we can always escape, mentally, from where we physically are. We may never really be there, in terms of our immediate experiences. And yet, one of the joys of travel is to explore the unknown. If we reply too heavily on digital previews, real-time dynamic maps with predefined routes and labels, and so on, we lose the opportunity to stumble on something rewarding, by chance. But we also remove the possibility of getting lost, and often reduce the level of danger we may expose ourselves to in risky neighbourhoods. From this we can see that digital travel lacks, and probably always will lack, the open elements of the unexpected that some would say is essential to real travel (e.g. Leed, 1991).

For the future, we plan to explore more ways of blending features from the universe of travel and that of technical devices and their interaction possibilities. For example, the metaphor "My phone is my home" is intriguing, due to the apparent contradiction of a device that permits contact with other people and places around the world becoming the safe haven to be returned to during travels in the physical world. An alternative metaphor would be "My phone is an extra set of eyes and ears that allow me to see and hear distant people and places". More generally, we believe that the impact of the level of presence experienced during digital travel will become more recognised and significant, including as a factor to deliberately consider during the design process. Selectable, or automatically variable, presence would seem to be a necessary feature, to balance the need for vivid experiences of other places with the needs of attending to significant events in the physical world.

Digital technology is used more and more in our society today, for everyday tasks, in gaming and entertainment and especially for communication at a distance. Technological development continues rapidly, but there is a need for more insight into the factors that support successful and satisfying interaction at a distance. In games and in movies we can see examples of what we might see in the future as consumer technology and in professional use. Movies and games have a story, a narrative, and we suggest that it is also partly due to there being a good story that we can have a real travel experience. It was noteworthy that some participants experiencing virtual sightseeing in our Los Angeles study felt the experience to be similar to visiting the actual place.

Many questions remain, but we believe that the physical and the virtual *can* be blended to support embodied interaction in integrated digital places. If digital places can become the object of real visits for participants, not only in the moment, but as lasting, memorable experiences of being there, subjectively real virtual travel could replace the disjointed social interactions through the Internet with which we have all become so familiar. In them, it should be possible to maintain role-sensitive social aspects of communication and behaviour.

Technology can be seen as taking us out into the world, to distant places. But it also brings the world to us, to our devices. Will we leave home to navigate, discover and experience distant digital worlds; worlds that we experience as reality? Or will the distinction between home and digital worlds disappear, as we carry with us the means to access distant people and places at any time, and from everywhere we go?

References

Ahn, S. J., & Bailenson, J. N. (2011). Self-endorsing versus other-endorsing in virtual environments. *Journal of Advertising, 40*(2), 93–106. https://doi.org/10.2753/JOA0091-3367400207

Bailenson, J. N. (2021). Nonverbal overload: A theoretical argument for the causes of Zoom fatigue. *Technology, Mind, and Behavior, 2*(1). https://doi.org/10.1037/tmb0000030

Cohen, E. (1979). Rethinking the sociology of tourism. *Annals of Tourism Research, 6*(1), 18–35. https://doi.org/10.1016/0160-7383(79)90092-6

Cui, G., Lockee, B., & Meng, C. (2013). Building modern online social presence: A review of social presence theory and its instructional design implications for future trends. *Education and Information Technologies, 18*(4), 661–685. https://doi.org/10.1007/s10639-012-9192-1

Fauconnier, G., & Turner, M. (1998). Conceptual integration networks. *Cognitive Science, 22*(2), 133–187. https://doi.org/10.1207/s15516709cog2202_1

Fauville, G., Luo, M., Queiroz, A. C. M., Bailenson, J. N., & Hancock, J. (2021). Nonverbal mechanisms predict zoom fatigue and explain why women experience higher levels than men. *SSRN Electronic Journal*. https://doi.org/10.2139/ssrn.3820035

Gunawardena, C. N. (1995). Social presence theory and implications for interaction collaborative learning in computer conferences. *International Journal of Educational Telecommunications, 1*(2–3), 147–166.

Hirschman, E. C., & Holbrook, M. B. (1982). Hedonic consumption: Emerging concepts, methods and propositions. *Journal of Marketing, 46*(3), 92. https://doi.org/10.2307/1251707

Holbrook, M. B., & Hirschman, E. C. (1982). The Experiential aspects of consumption: Consumer fantasies, feelings, and fun. *Journal of Consumer Research, 9*(2), 132. https://doi.org/10.1086/208906

Imaz, M., & Benyon, D. (2006). *Designing with blends: Conceptual foundations of human-computer interaction and software engineering*. MIT Press. https://doi.org/10.7551/mitpress/2377.001.0001

Isabet, B., Pino, M., Lewis, M., Benveniste, S., & Rigaud, A.-S. (2021). Social telepresence robots: A narrative review of experiments involving older adults before and during the COVID-19 pandemic. *International Journal of Environmental Research and Public Health, 18*(7), 3597. https://doi.org/10.3390/ijerph18073597

Kahneman, D. (2002). *Daniel Kahneman—Prize Lecture*. https://www.nobelprize.org/prizes/economic-sciences/2002/kahneman/lecture/

Kristoffersson, A., Coradeschi, S., & Loutfi, A. (2013). A review of mobile robotic telepresence. *Advances in Human-Computer Interaction, 2013*, 1–17. https://doi.org/10.1155/2013/902316

Leed, E. J. (1991). *The mind of the traveler: From Gilgamesh to global tourism*. Basic books.

Lombard, M., & Ditton, T. (1997). At the heart of it all: The concept of presence. *Journal of Computer-Mediated Communication, 3*(2). https://doi.org/10.1111/j.1083-6101.1997.tb00072.x

Merleau-Ponty, M. (1962). *Phenomenology of perception* (1962 [Paris: Gallimard, 1945]). Routledge and Kegan Paul.

Meyrowitz, J. (1986). *No sense of place: The impact of electronic media on social behavior* (1. issued as an Oxford University Press paperback). Oxford University Press.

Relph, E. (1976). *Place and placelessness*. SAGE.

Riva, G. (1999). From technology to communication: Psycho-social issues in developing virtual environments. *Journal of Visual Languages & Computing*, *10*(1), 87–97. https://doi.org/10.1006/jvlc.1998.0110

Shakeri, H., & Neustaedter, C. (2019). Teledrone: Shared outdoor exploration using telepresence drones. In *Conference companion publication of the 2019 on computer supported cooperative work and social computing*, pp. 367–371. https://doi.org/10.1145/3311957.3359475

Short, J., Williams, E., & Bruce, C. (1976). *The social psychology of telecommunications*. Wiley.

Slater, M. (2009). Place illusion and plausibility can lead to realistic behaviour in immersive virtual environments. *Philosophical Transactions of the Royal Society b: Biological Sciences*, *364*(1535), 3549–3557. https://doi.org/10.1098/rstb.2009.0138

Stanovich, K. E., & West, R. F. (2000). Individual differences in reasoning: Implications for the rationality debate? *Behavioral and Brain Sciences*, *23*(5), 645–665. https://doi.org/10.1017/S0140525X00003435

Timmins, L. R., & Lombard, M. (2005). When "Real" seems mediated: Inverse presence. *Presence: Teleoperators and Virtual Environments*, *14*(4), 492–500.

Tsui, K. M., Desai, M., Yanco, H. A., & Uhlik, C. (2011). Exploring use cases for telepresence robots. In *Proceedings of the 6th international conference on human-robot interaction—HRI '11*, 11. https://doi.org/10.1145/1957656.1957664

Turner, P. (2016). Making-believe with technology. In P. Turner (Ed.), *HCI Redux* (pp. 131–149). Springer International Publishing. https://doi.org/10.1007/978-3-319-42235-0_8

Turner, S., Huang, C.-W., Burrows, L., & Turner, P. (2016). Make-believing virtual realities. In P. Turner & J. T. Harviainen (Eds.), *Digital make-believe* (pp. 27–47). Springer International Publishing. https://doi.org/10.1007/978-3-319-29553-4_3

Waterworth, J. A. (1985). Why is synthetic speech harder to remember than natural speech? In *Proceedings of the SIGCHI conference on human factors in computing systems—CHI '85*, 201–206. https://doi.org/10.1145/317456.317493

Waterworth, J. A., Chignell, M., & Moller, H. (2020). Age-sensitive well-being support. In *Technology and health* (pp. 67–88). Elsevier. https://doi.org/10.1016/B978-0-12-816958-2.00004-6

Waterworth, J. A., Waterworth, E. L., Riva, G., & Mantovani, F. (2015). Presence: Form, content and consciousness. In M. Lombard, F. Biocca,

J. Freeman, W. IJsselsteijn, & R. J. Schaevitz (Eds.), *Immersed in media* (pp. 35–58). Springer International Publishing. https://doi.org/10.1007/978-3-319-10190-3_3

Waterworth, J., & Hoshi, K. (2016). Human-experiential design of presence in everyday blended reality. *Springer International Publishing*. https://doi.org/10.1007/978-3-319-30334-5

Wired. (2021). Google's Project Starline videoconference tech wants to turn you into a Hologram. Lauren Goode (journalist), May 18, 2021. https://www.wired.com/story/google-project-starline/

Open Access This chapter is licensed under the terms of the Creative Commons Attribution 4.0 International License (http://creativecommons.org/licenses/by/4.0/), which permits use, sharing, adaptation, distribution and reproduction in any medium or format, as long as you give appropriate credit to the original author(s) and the source, provide a link to the Creative Commons license and indicate if changes were made.

The images or other third party material in this chapter are included in the chapter's Creative Commons license, unless indicated otherwise in a credit line to the material. If material is not included in the chapter's Creative Commons license and your intended use is not permitted by statutory regulation or exceeds the permitted use, you will need to obtain permission directly from the copyright holder.

Index

A
Action, 96
Activities, 115
Advergames, 79
Advertising, 113
Affordance-action loop, 66
Affordances, 65, 96, 141
Anticipation, 135
Arrival, 4, 130
Attention, 62
Attractions, 113
Audio guide, 100

B
Behavioural intentions, 103
Behavioural outsideness, 102
Being *at a distance*, 52
Being there, 6, 18, 39, 56, 80
Belief, 56
Benogo project, 7
Blended everyday realities, 137
Blends, 136
Blind man's cane, 36
Breaks in presence, 39

C
Cognitive load of digital meetings, 131
Computer games, 2
Constructivist theory, 60
Covid-19 pandemic, 2, 129, 132
Cross-space mapping, 137

D
"Death of proximity", 3
Departure, 4, 130
Designing with blends, 136
Digital meetings, 107
Digital place, 78
Digital travel, 67
Digital travel applications, 113, 117
Digital travellers, 4, 120, 142
Digital travel survey, 96
Direct perception, 38
Disjunctivism, 21
Driver: San Francisco, 99
Dual process theories, 29

E

Embodied cognition, 39
Embodied interaction, 144
Embodiment, 31, 35
Emergent space, 136
Enactivism, 22, 64, 140
Everyday blended reality, 136
Experience, 15
"Experience economy", 16

F

Face-to-face, 130
Fictional realities, 57
First-person perspective, 14, 100
Full-body tracking, 134
Future of travel, 94

G

Gangs of London, 97
Generic space, 137
Geographical consciousness, 76
Glass metaphor, sheet of, 19
Google street view, 111
Grand Theft Auto, 6
Guest-host interaction, 106
Guided tours, 113, 117

H

Hallucination, 68, 141
Head-mounted display, 133
Hedonic consumption, 78, 104, 142
Hedonistic consumption, 94
Holidays, 109
Hollywood Audio Tour, 100
Hollywood Boulevard, 100
Holograms, 134
"Home-away-back-home" metaphor, 8, 135
Hosts, 105
Hotels, 113
Human-computer interaction (HCI), 32
Human geography, 76, 105

I

Illusion, 20, 58
The Illusion of non-mediation, 15, 55
Image schemata, 61
Imagination, 61, 68, 141
Indirect realism, 20, 26
Innate structures, 61
Insideness, 102
Insideness-outsideness, 76
Intention, 80
Introspection, 22
Intuitive judgment, 29
Inverse presence, 143

J

Journey, 4, 74

L

Life simulations, 98
Lived body, 77
Los Angeles, 98

M

Make-believing, 56
Marketing, 113, 142
Mediated presence, 52
Meetings, 139
Memorability for digital communication, 131
Memory, 68, 141
Metaphor, 136
Midnight Club LA, 98, 100
Mind-body problem, 17, 38
Mirrors, 64
Misperception, 60, 61

Mobile phones, 3
Müller-Lyer illusion, 59
Museums, 113, 117
"My phone is my home", 143

N
Naïve realism, 22
Narrative, 100, 144
Non-mediation, illusion of, 80
Nonverbal overload, 130

O
Outsideness, 83, 102

P
Passage, 4, 130
Perceived realness, 142
Perceptible affordance, 53, 65
Perception, 60
Perceptual experience, 16
Perceptual illusions, 58
Perceptual presence, 24
Phenomenological illusions, 58
Phenomenology, 37
Place, 142
Place and Placelessness (1976), 76
Place attachment, 76, 142
Place illusion, 57
Placeness, 102
Place theory, 105
Plausibility illusion, 57
Preparation, 135
Presence, 38, 52, 134
Presence as make-believe, 57
Presence in the world, 14
Present-at-hand, 32
Pretending, 56
Project Gotham Racing 4, 97
Psychophysical illusions, 58

R
Rapid acceptance response, 29
Ready-to-hand, 32
Realism, 98
Realistic semblance, 58
Recollection, 135
Relationalism, 140
Relationism, 18, 21
Representationalism, 18, 140
Residents, 102

S
The Sense-data view, 24
Sense of place, 74, 94
Sensorimotor approach to perception, 24
Sharing, 135
Sightseeing, 66, 97, 102, 104
Simulation, 57
Sinister watcher, 60
Social drones, 132
Social presence, 8, 53, 63, 131
Social Presence Theory (SPT), 64
Social telepresence robots, 132
Socio-psychological needs, 139
Spaces and places, 75
Stories, 99
Structural coupling, 39
Surrogate action, 132
Surrogate body, 59
System 1 and System 2, 15, 29

T
"Take place", 130
Technologically-mediated experiences, 34
Teleconferencing, 131
Telepresence, 7, 33, 94, 141
Telepresence: being present at a distance, 55
Telepresence Experience Survey, 7

Telepresence presence, 52
Temple Presence Inventory, 98, 101
Time lag between exchanges, 131
Tools, 31
Top-down processing, 61
Tourism, 4, 66, 76, 142
Tourism experience, 76, 82
Tourism marketing, 78
Tourist gaze, 5
Transparency, 31, 34, 55, 140
Travel experience, 95
Travel products, 113
Travel services, 111
Type-1 cognitive process, 57
Type-1 processing, 82
Type-2 cognitive process, 57
Type-2 processing, 82

U
Usability studies, 32

V
Vacation, 109
Vacation planning, 94
Vicarious experiences, 81
Vicarious outsideness, 102
Videoconferencing, 2
Video game, 6, 97
Virtual Reality (VR), 53
Virtual tourism, 5, 6, 94
Visual experience, 19
VR for tourism, 5

W
Willingness to pay, 120
Word of mouth (WoM), 80

Z
Zoom fatigue, 130

The manufacturer's authorised representative in the EU is Springer Nature Customer Service Centre GmbH, Europaplatz 3, 69115 Heidelberg, Germany. If you have any concerns regarding our products, please contact ProductSafety@springernature.com

Printed and bound by CPI Group (UK) Ltd, Croydon, CR0 4YY

25/03/2026

02078175-0014